Immigration and the Future of Canadian Society

S.D. Clark

The University of Toronto's Department of Sociology was established in 1963. Samuel Delbert (S.D.) Clark (1910–2003) was its founding chair.

Clark was born in Lloydmister, Alberta, and attended the University of Saskatchewan, the London School of Economics, McGill University and the University of Toronto. He analyzed the transformation of successive Canadian frontiers from socially disorganized settlements into organized societies. He then conducted research on how economic change in Canada resulted in inequality as reflected in patterns of residential segregation. His books include *The Canadian Manufacturers Association* (1939), *The Social Development of Canada* (1942), *Church and Sect in Canada* (1948), *Movements of Political Protest in Canada* (1959), *The Developing Canadian Community* (1962), *The Suburban Society* (1966), *Canadian Society in Historical Perspective* (1976) and *The New Urban Poor* (1978).

Clark served as president of the Canadian Political Science Association, honorary president of the Canadian Sociology and Anthropology Association and president of the Royal Society of Canada. He was awarded the J.B. Tyrell Historical Medal, became a foreign honorary member of the American Academy of Arts and Sciences and an Officer of the Order of Canada, and received honorary degrees from half a dozen Canadian universities.

In 1999, Clark's son, William Edmund (Ed) Clark, endowed the S.D. Clark Chair in Sociology at the University of Toronto in honour of his father.

Immigration and the Future of Canadian Society

PROCEEDINGS OF THE SECOND S.D. CLARK SYMPOSIUM ON THE FUTURE OF CANADIAN SOCIETY

EDITED BY
Robert Brym

Rock's Mills Press
Oakville, Ontario
2017

PUBLISHED BY
ROCK'S MILLS PRESS
www.rocksmillspress.com

Copyright © 2017 by Robert Brym
All rights reserved. Published by arrangement with the editor.

A portion of the royalties from the sale of this book will be donated to the Canadian Red Cross, which provides independent monitoring of detention facilities holding immigration detainees, thus promoting a protective environment in which detainees are treated humanely and where their human rights and dignity are respected.

Cover: Two asylum seekers climb through deep snow at the Canada-United States border on their way from North Dakota to Emerson, Manitoba. Like all such migrants, they were detained, processed, and released to await a decision on whether they would be granted refugee status. Photo credit: Ian Willms.

For information, contact customer.service@rocksmillspress.com.
Library and Archives Canada Cataloguing in Publication data is available from the publisher.

Contents

INTRODUCTION
1. Immigration and the Future of Canadian Society 1
   Robert Brym

PART ONE: COMPARATIVE PERSPECTIVES.. 10

2. Immigration and Mainstream Expansion in Canada and the United States 11
   Richard Alba
3. Multicultural Nation-building and Canada's Future: Implications of Comparative Research 30
   Jeffrey G. Reitz
4. Race, Religion, and Citizenship Capital: Comment on Alba and Reitz .. 50
   Naomi Lightman

PART TWO: ISSUES IN CANADIAN IMMIGRATION 57

5. Second Generation Educational and Occupational Attainment in Canada 58
   Monica Boyd
6. Immigration, Precarious Noncitizenship, and the Changing Landscape of Work 81
   Patricia Landolt
7. On the Role of Race and Gender in the Study of Migrant Adaptation in Canada: Comment on Boyd and Landolt 105
   Salina Abji

Contributors 109

Index 111

List of Tables

2.1. Growing Diversity at the Top of the Workforce: Non-Hispanic White Percentage of Top Occupational Quartile by Birth Cohort, United States, 2000 and 2010 19
2.2. Mixed Unions in the Second Generation by Group, Canada and the United States, in percent 21
5.1. Regression of Holding High-Skill Occupation on Demographic and Educational Predictors, Canada, 2011 72
5.2. Regression of Average Occupational Score on Demographic and Educational Predictors, Canada, 2011 74
6.1. Temporary Foreign Workers by Urban Area and Province/Territory, 2015-16 95

List of Figures

2.1. Canada's Visible Minority Population by Age, 2006 (Measured) and 2031 (Projected) 17
3.1. National Values of Immigrant Inclusion and Exclusion 36
3.2. Regression of Preference for More Immigrants on Predictors 37
3.3. Experience of Discrimination by Religion and Origin 39
5.1. Percentage with Bachelor's Degree or Higher, 2nd and 3rd-plus Generations by Age, Population Age 25-64, Canada, 2011 62
5.2. Percentage with Bachelor's Degree or Higher by Generation and Visible Minority Status, Age 25-39, Canada, 2011 64
5.3. Percentage with No Postsecondary Degree by Generation and Visible Minority Status, Age 25-39, Canada, 2011 65
6.1. Permanent and Temporary Immigration, 1983-2012 90
6.2. Temporary Migration Stock and Flow, 1983-2012 90
6.3. Types of Permanent Immigration, 2003-2012 91

Immigration and the Future of Canadian Society

INTRODUCTION

CHAPTER ONE
Immigration and the Future of Canadian Society

Robert Brym

Immigration as Politics
A spectre is haunting Europe and the United States—the spectre of immigration. It has awakened terrifying demons that go by the name of Le Pen in France, Farage in the UK, Trump in the United States, Wilders in the Netherlands, Salvini in Italy, Hofer in Austria, Jobbik in Hungary, the Kaczynski twins in Poland, and Petry and Meuthen in Germany. Traditional parties are seeking to exorcise these demons but the demons grow more powerful nonetheless, demanding sturdier barriers to new immigration and the expulsion of recent and, in some cases, not-so-recent arrivals.

Only Canada seems to stand apart (Ibbitson 2016). *The Economist* made it official on the cover of a late 2016 issue, trumpeting, among our other virtues, the warmth of our welcome to immigrants ("The last liberals" 2016; "Liberty moves north" 2016). And *The Economist* is not alone. For the past seven years, the Reputation Institute, an international consulting company, has conducted an annual survey of a representative sample of nearly 60,000 people worldwide (Reputation Institute 2016). One of their key measures of a country's reputation is based on responses to questions regarding how welcoming respondents consider the country. In four of the past seven years, Canada ranked first in reputation worldwide. In the other three years, Canada ranked second. And why not? The federal Conservative governments' disinterest in Syrian refugees helped to defeat them in 2015. We lack a nationwide anti-immigration movement of any significance, let alone a party. Between July 2015 and July 2016 Canada welcomed 320,932 immigrants— the largest annual number of new arrivals in the country's history, proportionately more than in any year since 1911, and proportionately 60 percent more than the number welcomed by the United

States. In November 2016, the federal government increased the desired annual rate of immigration by 20 percent to 300,000. Some members of the Liberal government, including the Minister of Immigration, want it to be set even higher (CIC News 2016).

And yet, from a different point of view, Canada does not so much stand apart as it remains (perhaps characteristically) a little behind the times. A 2016 poll found that 68 per cent of Canadians think ethnic and racial minorities should be doing more to fit in with mainstream society. The corresponding percentage in the United States was 53 percent (Angus Reid Institute 2016). The rate of upward mobility of Canadian immigrants slowed about 25 years ago and remains at historically low levels (Reitz 2011). Children of immigrants report significantly more prejudice and discrimination than their parents do (Reitz and Banerjee 2007). Is it possible that the situation of Canadians immigrants (or at least some categories of Canadian immigrants) and the attitudes of Canadians toward immigration are less rosy than many of us are prepared to believe?

What can be said with certainty is that economic forces much like those that engendered Trumpism in the United States and Brexitism in the UK are operating here, heightening ethnic and racial competition for jobs. Freer investment and trade have contributed to a polarization of the class structure by rewarding the wealthy and the highly educated while facilitating the flow of hundreds of thousands of well-paying manufacturing jobs to low-wage jurisdictions, only to be replaced here by low-paying, often part-time service jobs. CIBC economists have documented the trend; their measure of the average quality of Canadian jobs fell 13 percent between 1988 and 2015 (Tal 2015). This means that you stand a pretty good chance of finding the woman who once worked full-time on the General Motors assembly line now scanning made-in-China products part-time at the Walmart checkout counter for half the hourly wage and no benefits.

True, Canada's welfare state has provided a stronger safety net than has the welfare state in the United States. That may be why organized discontent over the perceived competition of immigrants on the job market is more muted here. However, the economic security of the dispossessed is not assured. Personal and provincial government debt stands at record highs, while the federal debt-to-GDP ratio rose 38 percent from 2007 to 2016. While the unemployment rate has fallen from its recent highs, the labour force participation rate is also declining. Fear of peak oil supply has become fear of peak oil demand. Monetary policy is unable to stimulate growth. A real estate correction could bleed into the larger economy. Even ignoring the possibility of foreign shocks, these domestic warning signs suggest that a Paul Martin-magnitude welfare state retrenchment is not out of the question. If the safety net weakens, it is possible that some Canadians' attitude toward immigrants will become significantly more hostile and organized.

Some leaders are certainly ready for that eventuality. In October 2016, Jean-François Lisée won the Parti Québécois leadership on a platform of reducing immigration levels and banning the *burka* in public. Quebec's ruling Liberal government held hearings on proposed legislation that would make it illegal to give or receive government services if a person's face is covered (Peritz 2016; Perreaux 2016). Kellie Leitch, a contender (albeit an unsuccessful one) for the federal Conservative Party leadership, announced during the 2015 federal election campaign her support for an RCMP tip line where Canadians could report what she called "barbaric cultural practices." In April 2016 she suggested that it might be a good idea to vet would-be immigrants and refugees for so-called "anti-Canadian values" (Tunney 2016).

Canadian Immigration in Comparative Perspective

The papers in this collection help us better understand Canadian immigration policy by placing it in comparative perspective and identifying blind spots in Canadian immigration analysis and policymaking.

Richard Alba leads off by examining the assimilation of a growing number of immigrants' descendants into the Canadian and American mainstreams. He defines assimilation broadly as "the decline of an ethnic distinction and its corollary cultural and social differences." This definition recognizes that assimilation may be accompanied by (1) change in ethno-racial differences and identities on the part of minorities *and* the majority; and (2) the *persistence* of some ethno-racial distinctions on the part of minorities. For Alba, the endpoint of assimilation is not the disappearance of minority groups but the incorporation of the descendants of minority-group immigrants into the mainstream to the point where they feel at home there. Importantly, however, the mainstream becomes socially and culturally heterogeneous as it incorporates these new recruits.

The decades following World War II witnessed the incorporation of Jewish and Catholic minorities in the Canadian and American mainstreams. Intermarriage became commonplace. Mainstream identity in the United States became "Judeo-Christian" while mainstream identity in Canada became "multicultural." Today, assimilation into the mainstream continues as members of the mainly White, baby-boom generation retire and the descendants of immigrants, many of them non-Whites of non-European heritage, enter vacated positions. Alba's survey of demographic, labour-force, and intermarriage data forecasts a far-reaching transformation of the Canadian and American mainstreams over the next few decades. According to Alba, only Americans of African descent, victims of slavery and ongoing racism, will be substantially left out of the mainstream, although Monica Boyd's chapter later in this volume shows that many Black, Arab, and visible-minority Canadians of Latin-American descent may face similar problems when it comes to occupational attainment.[1]

Jeff Reitz shifts our attention from Canadian/American comparisons of the mainstream to the comparative analysis of attitudes toward immigration and social inclusion/exclusion in France, Québec, and the rest of Canada. He aims to explain why Canadians have a comparatively positive attitude toward immigration and relative success with immigrant integration. He asks: What factors lie beneath our relative tolerance, inclusiveness, and openness to multiculturalism? He finds the answer in certain geopolitical, historical, and economic circumstances.

The threat of Québec separatism in the 1960s encouraged the official declaration of Canada as a bilingual and bicultural country. The resulting sense of exclusion on the part of immigrant groups led to the adoption of a multicultural policy in the early 1970s. By

---

1. Indigenous people are not immigrants, but it may be noted parenthetically that relatively few of them are likely to become part of the mainstream in the next few decades because of the legacy of colonialism and persistent racism.

comparison, the United States faced two difficulties that diverted the country from multiculturalism: a history of slavery, which caused it to inherit racist institutions and attitudes, and a southern border with Mexico that made uncontrolled migration possible. Similarly, Western Europe permitted largely unregulated post-colonial immigration. In contrast, Canada adopted a policy of selecting immigrants based largely on their economic utility. We tended to choose immigrants who were likely to experience rapid upward mobility while Western Europe did not, making our record with immigrant integration superior.

Reitz next shows that socio-economic differences between France, Québec, and the rest of Canada are largely responsible for differences in the degree of integration of Muslim immigrants in the three settings. With respect to attitudes to immigration, he finds little to distinguish Québec from the rest of Canada but much to differentiate Canada as a whole from France. However, the more negative French attitude is due largely to negative perceptions of the economic value of immigration, not negative attitudes toward multiculturalism or religion per se. Other findings support the view that the key to immigrant integration lies less in culture than in socio-economic realities. For example, Reitz finds that race, not religion, is largely responsible for variation in Muslim immigrants' perceptions of discrimination; White Muslims perceive relatively little discrimination. The level of stress experienced by Muslim immigrants is associated with unemployment and labour market inactivity, not strength of religious attachment. Larger Muslim economic disadvantages in France than in Canada are due mainly to such factors as the lower average level of education of French Muslims compared to their Canadian counterparts. These and related findings support the conclusion that differences between settings in social values related to multiculturalism and religion are (1) smaller than they seem and (2) depend mainly on the economic characteristics of immigrants. It follows that Canada's uniqueness lies in our relatively strict control over immigration processes and our capacity to ensure the upward mobility of immigrants. The lessons for social policy are clear.

Naomi Lightman augments the analyses of Alba and Reitz by noting that, in addition to race and religion, "citizenship capital" is an increasingly important basis of social exclusion. She defines citizenship capital as "the myriad ways that migration trajectories and legal statuses may lead to the dispossession and devaluation of financial, social, and cultural capital." According to Lightman, citizenship capital is an increasingly important axis of social exclusion because the number of illegalized, non-permanent, and refugee migrants is rising so rapidly worldwide. It is likely, she claims, that analyzing the citizenship capital of migrants may well produce evidence of a growing social divide in addition to, and intersecting with, race and religion. She concludes by challenging researchers to study this largely unmeasured basis of social exclusion, a challenge that Patricia Landolt takes up later in this volume.

Issues in Canadian Immigration

The second part of this volume focuses on two key issues in the study of Canadian immigration: the educational and occupational achievement of second-generation Canadians and the increasingly large number of Canadians residents whose status is well described as that of "precarious noncitizenship."

Monica Boyd analyzes how the second generation has been doing educationally and occupationally compared to the third generation and beyond, distinguishing among the trajectories followed by different visible-minority groups. She also examines the sociological factors that account for diverse trajectories. With respect to the first issue, Boyd finds that the second generation does better than the third-plus generation. She adduces several reasons for this finding. Second-generation descendants of immigrants are more highly concentrated in large urban centres with relatively abundant educational and job opportunities than are their third-plus generation counterparts. Moreover, immigrant parents are relatively highly educated and this circumstance influences the educational outcomes of their children more than the educational outcomes of their grandchildren. Beyond that, immigrant parents tend to have extraordinarily high expectations for the educational attainment of their children. However, important variations by race exist.

In 2011, all but two visible-minority groups of young Canadians (ages 25-39) attained a higher level of education than did members of the White third-plus generation. On average, Blacks attained the same level of education as did members of the White third-plus generation. Latin Americans attained a significantly lower level of education. The picture for occupational attainment and earnings differs somewhat. For example, in 2011, after taking demographic and educational characteristics into account, young second generation Canadians of Arab, Latin American, and Black heritage attained significantly lower occupational scores than did members of the White third-plus generation. Having eliminated the possibility that these differences are due to demographic and educational factors, there remains the possibility that the significantly lower occupational attainment of these groups is due to labour force discrimination.[2]

According to Patricia Landolt, precarious noncitizenship acts as another barrier to the upward mobility and integration of some migrants to Canada, and an increasingly important one at that. Developing Lightman's earlier admonition concerning citizenship capital, Landolt demonstrates that changes to our immigration system over the last few decades have substantially increased the inflow of temporary noncitizen migrants to Canada. By 2012, more than a million Canadian residents were temporary noncitizens—about 3 percent of the resident population, up from about 1 percent in 1983. Some temporary noncitizens eventually become citizens. Others do not. Among the latter are several hundred thousand people who have remained in the country without legal status.

Nearly all adult temporary noncitizens enter the labour market, where the great majority of them suffer a variety of depredations including wage robbery, abuse, and labour immobility. Landolt analyzes the impediments faced by temporary noncitizens with diverse immigration statuses. Among other things, she finds that temporary noncitizen status exerts an enduring, negative impact on occupational and income attainment even among people who eventually win citizenship.

---

2. Canadian employers confronted with job applicants who appear to differ only in their apparent race or country of origin are more likely to call back or make job offers to applicants who are not members of visible minority groups (Dechief and Oreopoulos 2012; Henry and Ginzberg 1985). However, research has not yet demonstrated whether some visible-minority groups are less likely than others are to receive call-backs or job offers. Note also that Boyd's findings regarding occupational scores rely on highly aggregated occupational categories and are not found in her analysis of the percentage of people holding high-skill occupations.

Salina Abji concludes the volume by underscoring the need to study interaction effects when analyzing the life-chances of immigrants in Canada. Other authors in this volume examine the independent effects of race, religion, and citizenship status on the status attainment and social integration of immigrants. By offering illustrations of the way these factors interact with each other and with gender, Abji challenges researchers to uncover a potentially more complex and revealing picture of immigrant adaptation and non-adaptation in Canada.

Taken together, the authors of this volume give ample reason for both optimism and pessimism about the future of immigration in Canadian society. On the optimistic side, they give us to understand that upward mobility has historically been a well-trod path into the changing mainstream—and continues to be just that for most immigrant groups. On the pessimistic side, they adduce evidence consistent with the view that some immigrant groups face labour force discrimination and obdurate legal barriers to full citizenship that prevent them from becoming well integrated in Canadian society. The saving grace in this picture may be a hard demographic reality. An aging Canadian population requiring more pension assistance and medical care cannot live securely without a substantial and growing influx of young, energetic, well-educated, tax-paying immigrants. Widespread recognition of this fact leading to appropriate social policy may be the best insurance against racial and religious discrimination by Canadian-born citizens and the malintegration of some immigrant groups in Canadian society.

References

Angus Reid Institute. 2016. "What makes us Canadian? A study of values, beliefs, priorities and identity." http://angusreid.org/canada-values/.
CIC News. 2016. "Canada Welcomed a Record 320,932 New Immigrants over the Past Year, with Immigration Numbers Set to Increase Even Further." http://www.cicnews.com/2016/09/canada-welcomed-record-320932-new-immigrants-immigration-numbers-set-increase-098533.html.
Dechief, Diane and Philip Oreopoulos. 2012. "Why do some employers prefer to interview Matthew but not Samir? New evidence from Toronto, Montreal and Vancouver." Canadian Labour Market and Skills Researcher Network Working Paper No. 95. March. http://www.clsrn.econ.ubc.ca/workingpapers/CLSRN%20Working%20Paper%20no.%2095%20-%20Dechief%20 and%20Oreopoulos.pdf.
Goodman, Peter. 2016. "More Wealth, More Jobs, but Not for Everyone: What Fuels the Backlash on Trade." *New York Times*, 28 September. http://www.nytimes.com/2016/09/29/business/economy/more-wealth-more-jobs-but-not-for-everyone-what-fuels-the-backlash-on-trade.html
Henry, Frances and Effie Ginzberg. 1985. "Who Gets the Work? A Test of Racial Discrimination in Employment." Toronto: Urban Alliance on Race Relations and the Social Planning Council of Metropolitan Toronto. https://urbanalliance.files.wordpress.com/2012/05/who-gets-the-work.pdf.
Ibbitson, John. 2016. "In a world of closing doors, Canada is embracing inclusion." *Globe and Mail*, 1 July. http://www.theglobeandmail.com/news/national/in-a-world-of-closing-doors-canada-is-embracing-inclusion/article30731700/.
"The last liberals: Canada." *The Economist*, 28 October – 4 November. http://www.economist.com/news/briefing/21709291-why-canada-still-ease-openness-last-liberals.
"Liberty moves north: Canada's example to the world." *The Economist*, 28 October-4 November. http://www.economist.com/news/leaders/21709305-it-uniquely-fortunate-many-waysbut-canada-still-holds-lessons-other-western.
Peritz, Ingrid. 2016. "Hearings to begin on proposed Quebec law targeting veiled women." *Globe and Mail*, 18 October. http://www.theglobeandmail.com/news/national/hearings-to-begin-on-proposed-quebec-law-targeting-veiled-women/article32403990/.
Perreaux, Les. 2016. "Jean-François Lisée brings identity politics back to Parti Québécois." *Globe and Mail*, 9 October. http://www.theglobeandmail.com/news/national/jean-francois-lisee-brings-identity-politics-back-to-parti-quebecois/article32312570/.
Reitz, Jeffrey G. 2011. "Tapping Immigrants' Skills." Pp. 178-93 in Robert Brym, ed. *Society in Question*, 6th ed. Toronto: Nelson.
Reitz, Jeffrey G. and Rupa Banerjee. 2007. "Racial Inequality, Social Cohesion and Policy Issues in Canada." Pp. 489-545 in Keith Banting, Thomas J. Courchene, and F. Leslie Seidle, eds. *Belonging? Diversity, Recognition and Shared Citizenship in Canada*. Montreal: Institute for Research on Public Policy.
Reputation Institute. 2016. "2016 Country RepTrak®: The Most Reputable Countries in the World." https://www.reputationinstitute.com/CMSPages/GetAzureFile.aspx?path=~\media\media\documents\country-reptrak-2016.pdf&hash=5a4232c6bfda0af12fca90660d5f8d18a657ac230d062e34e0bb-589c0d3c1538&ext=.pdf.
Tal, Benjamin. 2015. "Employment Quality—Trending Down." CIBC Canadian Employment Quality Index. http://research.cibcwm.com/economic_public/download/eqi_20150305.pdf.
Tunney, Catharine. 2016. "Kellie Leitch defends 'anti-Canadian values' survey question." CBC News 2 September. http://www.cbc.ca/news/politics/leitch-responds-survey-question-1.3746470.

Part One
COMPARATIVE PERSPECTIVES

CHAPTER TWO
Immigration and Mainstream Expansion in Canada and the United States

Richard Alba

Introduction
Assimilation processes are at work in Canada and the United States, bringing descendants of immigrants into societal mainstreams and thereby altering not just the profiles of immigrant-origin groups but also the mainstreams themselves. This does not mean that assimilation is the only story—in the United States and, to a lesser extent, Canada, where social cleavages between Whites and non-Whites remain profoundly important, disadvantages for the children of immigrants rooted in the institutionalized hierarchy of ethnicity and race remain consequential. So, too, are the disadvantages originating in the lack of legal status of some immigrant parents, which has been shown to limit the life chances of even their U.S.-born, and hence U.S.-citizen, children (Bean et al. 2015). Yet whatever the level of persisting inequality and distinction between native majorities and immigrant-origin groups, the penetration of growing numbers of the second and third generations into the mainstream is an important development with potential implications for the long-run evolution of these societies. To develop this argument, I consider the concept of assimilation that can best help us to understand this development; the assimilation histories of Canada and the United States that provide clues to the present; the evidence of mainstream expansion; and its significance.

Assimilation and the Mainstream
Canadian and American social scientists are not in agreement on the fundamental concept that should be used to investigate the incorporation of immigrant groups in receiving societies. In Canada, "integration" is favoured, whereas south of the border, "assimila-

tion" is still widely used (Alba et al. 2012; Kymlicka 2010; Li 2003). The differences between these two notions can be exaggerated but they do differ in one critical respect relevant to an understanding of mainstream expansion. "Integration" usually refers to the processes that increase the opportunities of immigrants and their descendants to obtain the valued rewards of a society, as well as social acceptance, through participation in major institutions such as the educational and political system and the labour and housing markets. "Assimilation" includes these processes and others involved in cultural change ("acculturation"), ultimately resulting in social amalgamation with the dominant majority population (Alba and Nee 2003; Alba and Foner 2015). Indeed, the notion of assimilation hypothesizes the existence of a relationship between integration and these other processes, though not one so hard-and-fast that we can presume a fixed causal direction between them.

Contemporary proponents of both concepts argue that the changes brought about by the processes to which they refer are, to some extent, two-sided; not just the immigrant groups but the mainstream society is changed by integration/assimilation. Of course, even if two-sided, change is likely to be asymmetric, with the immigrant groups changing more. Nevertheless, the notion that the mainstream also changes revises the canonical formulations that form the backdrop to contemporary ideas about integration and assimilation.

The assimilationist canon was most clearly laid out in Milton Gordon's (1964) classic volume. Gordon understood assimilation as a one-way adjustment by minority populations to the middle-class majority—White Protestant in the United States, in his view. He envisioned the endpoint of assimilation as a change of group membership; minority groups might, after they acquired the culture of the native majority and integrated socially with it, merge into the majority.

The neo-assimilation approach, which I will use here and is widely associated with *Remaking the American Mainstream* (Alba and Nee 2003), revises these ideas in fundamental respects. Its widely quoted definition equates assimilation with "the decline of an ethnic distinction and its corollary cultural and social differences" (Alba and Nee 2003: 11). This definition does not assume that assimilation involves only changes on the minority side or the elimination of ethno-racial differences and identities. Moreover, it allows that ethno-racial variations may persist even into advanced stages of assimilation, but in a muted form consistent with various forms of social integration with the dominant group.

The neo-assimilation approach also modifies the conception of assimilation's end-stage. Instead of the complete merger of the assimilating minority into the majority, it equates full assimilation with incorporation into a "mainstream." The idea of the mainstream is suited to an ethno-racially stratified society since the mainstream can be thought of as the home to the members of the dominant population. One way to imagine it is as the assemblage of social and cultural spaces where the presence of members of the dominant population is unremarkable or taken for granted. In the event, even if the mainstream is where the dominant majority is found "at home," it need not be exclusive. That is, individuals from outside the White majority can participate in mainstream settings and be accepted there. And the mainstream itself is internally quite diverse along various dimensions, such as social class and region, which are associated with heterogeneities in the majority population. One can speak meaningfully of mainstreams in the plural, not just the singular.

What Can We Learn from the North American History of Assimilation?[1]

If we want to understand what mainstream expansion looks like on the ground (as opposed to in the abstract), then we need only look to the immigration histories of Canada and the United States. This is an important exercise because it can dispel some simplistic ideas about assimilation—for example, the widely repeated trope that assimilation eliminates ethnic distinctions and eradicates cultural difference. It can also yield clues about what to look for as indicators of mainstream shift.

In looking to the past, we should also recognize the advantages that assimilation has bestowed on North American societies as compared to European societies such as France and Germany,

---

1. North America includes all 23 countries north of the Panama/Colombia border. However, for convenience, we use the term here to refer only to Canada and the United States.

which have also received many immigrants since the middle of the 20th century. These advantages accrue to Canada and the U.S. because they are settler societies. That is, they have been peopled mainly by immigrants and their descendants, and this history is enshrined in the founding myths of their nationhood. Because of the historical experience of needing to incorporate new immigrants from Europe rapidly, both societies have developed ways of quickly enfolding immigrants and their children in the embrace of the national identity. In Canada and the United States, large proportions of immigrants and their children identify with their countries of residence and feel at home there; these facts present a contrast to the relationship of European societies to their non-Western immigrants (Alba and Foner 2015: 198-207). In the case of Canada, the embrace of immigrants is strengthened by fairly easy access to citizenship (Bloemraad 2006); and in both North American countries, the second generation need not question its national membership because its members gain citizenship unconditionally at birth, a contrast to the citizenship provisions in much of Europe (Alba and Foner 2015: 146).

Canada and the United States have also experienced previous periods of large-scale mainstream expansion, suggesting that the mechanisms at work in this expansion, such as intermarriage, are embedded in their social orders and enjoy considerable legitimacy. The last such period—and the best remembered one—took place in the decades following World War II. It ushered in the Jewish and Catholic descendants of the most recent waves of European immigrants. In Canada, it also included the French. On the eve of World War II, the North American mainstreams were dominated by Protestant Whites, especially those from the British Isles (Baltzell 1964; Porter 1965; see also Alba 2009). By the last quarter of the 20th century, the core identities of these mainstreams had been transformed into a Judaeo-Christian identity in the case of the United States and into a multicultural identity in the case of Canada.

The mid-century expansion of the North American mainstreams, even though it was limited to Canadians and Americans of European ancestry, made the mainstreams more diverse. In Canada, French received the imprimatur of an official language, equal in governmental status to English. In both countries, Catholics and Jews not only gained recognition as full members of the mainstream, but their religions received their mainstream charters, as it were (Alba et al. 2007). Granted, the religions as practiced by most of their adherents evolved in ways that made them more compatible with mainstream values. For example, among Catholics, individualism of faith increased and was expressed as willingness to reject specific Church teachings. However, assimilation did not entail mass conversion to Protestantism. It is fair to conclude that expansion can involve growing diversity within the mainstream, as long as diversity is kept within certain bounds.

Several social forces contributed to the mass entry of the previously excluded groups into the mainstream. Take the case of the United States. Post-World War II mass assimilation took place in a period of unusual prosperity and low economic inequality. This economic setting allowed for what could be called "non-zero-sum" mobility. That is, the social ascent by individuals from ethnic minority backgrounds did not appear to hamper the opportunities available to those in the White Protestant majority. Consequently, minority mobility did not intensify competition along ethnic lines in a way that the boundary with the established majority was "brightened." The assimilatory effects of such factors as the shifting generational distribution of recent immigrant groups—at mid-century, the young adults from these groups belonged mainly to the second and third generations—were thereby enhanced. Combined with the cut-off of immigration since the 1920s, the transition to the post-immigration generations brought about rapid Americanization and the weakening of mother tongues. The educational attainments of low-status groups like the Italians soared after World War II (assisted, one should add, by state-sponsored expansion of higher education). Occupational mobility followed (Alba 2009; Perlmann 2005). The development of suburbs and homeownership encouraged young ethnic families to forsake urban enclaves for mixed communities.

As a consequence of these processes, rates of interethnic and interreligious marriage climbed. For example, as of the mid-1960s in the United States, 70 percent of the Italian-American third generation was marrying out (Alba and Nee 2003). Jews were the most sensitive barometer of these trends. From a rate that was initially low—around 10 percent circa 1950—the intermarriage rate of Jews soared to more than half by the end of the twentieth century (Fishman 2004). In effect, then, not only did the mainstreams become more internally diverse, so did families. The spread of intermarriage contributed to further erosion of ethnicity and religion, which is apparent in the shifts occurring among American Jews (Wertheimer and Cohen 2014).

One other consequence of mass assimilation is noteworthy—the persistence of ethnic identities in an attenuated, symbolic form (Gans 1979). The acceptance of hyphenated identities, such as Italian-American or -Canadian, was solidified by inclusion of groups with historically recent immigration backgrounds, whose members could not easily think of themselves solely in terms of North American identities. Hyphenation was not unknown in earlier eras, but was more controversial, as suggested by President Theodore Roosevelt's famous injunction to "swat the hyphen" (Gerstle 2001). This is another way that North American societies have developed inclusionary mechanisms without parallels in Europe.

Demographic Shift and Minority Social Mobility

If large-scale mainstream assimilation depends on non-zero-sum mobility, the scale of mainstream expansion is likely to be much less today than in the highly unusual post-World War II period. Economic inequality is higher today, especially in the United States, where social mobility appears to have declined in recent decades (Corak 2013). An additional impediment in the United States arises from the issue of legal status among immigrant parents, which was much less consequential in the past than it is today (Ngai 2003; Bean et al. 2015).

Nevertheless, assimilation processes still operate. One structural force that promotes them is demographic shift (Alba 2009). Both Canada and the United States have entered a profound, demographically driven transition to diversity, which is about to accelerate and will run to completion during the next two decades. The engine of this transition is a conjunction of two huge demographic forces: the aging of the baby boom and the entry into adulthood of massive second and even third generations issuing from immigration.

Figure 2.1. Canada's Visible Minority Population by Age, 2006 (Measured) and 2031 (Projected)

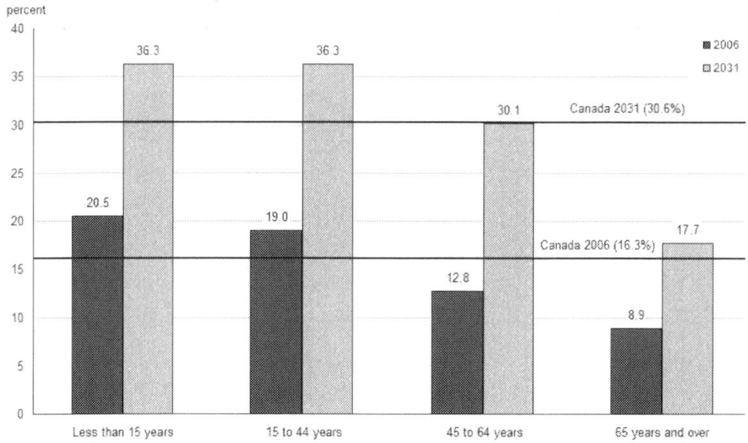

Age group	2006	2031
Less than 15 years	20.5	36.3
15 to 44 years	19.0	36.3
45 to 64 years	12.8	30.1
65 years and over	8.9	17.7

Canada 2006 (16.3%); Canada 2031 (30.6%)

Source: Statistics Canada (2010).

Members of the baby boom cohort were born during the two decades following World War II (conventionally dated as 1946-64/5). They are beginning to leave the ages of economic and civic activity. They belong largely to the native majority group, were the first to experience mass higher education, and occupy many high positions in the economy and civil society. Their departure will create many vacancies in the labour force and civil society. Moreover, the cohorts reaching the ages of labor-force entry, family formation, and civic participation, will look quite different—they will contain many more young adults who have been raised in immigrant homes and who are potentially disadvantaged as a consequence. The question that will have to be addressed in North America in the near future is: Who will replace the baby boomers?

Figure 2.1 indicates the dimensions of this transition in Canada. It shows the distribution of visible minorities in the recent past and, as projected by Statistics Canada, in the near future. As in the United States, the middle-aged population, representing the baby-boom cohorts, remains disproportionately White. Younger cohorts contain substantially larger fractions of minorities. In 2006, 20 percent of Canadian children under the age of 16 were members of visible minority groups. By 2031, the Canadian figure is projected to rise to more than a third, and the fraction of visible minority group members among young adults will be equally high.

In the United States, the transition to diversity is even more thorough-going. In 2016, nearly half of children (under the age of 18) were not White. The United States Census Bureau projects that Whites will cease to hold numerical majority status within three decades (Alba 2016). (However, even if Whites lose their numerical majority, they will still form a plurality; and they need not lose their majority status in the sociological sense of the term because they may still remain the dominant group, monopolizing social power.) There can be no doubt about the declining number of White majority group members in the working-age population. In 2010 the largest number of Whites was found in the baby-boom cohort (then aged 46-64). Among those who were 0-19 years old, the number of Whites was 23 percent smaller; and of course this age group represents the cohort that has entered or will enter the labour force during the 2010s, 2020s, and early 2030s. Thus, not only is the fraction of young people belonging to the White majority falling; so too is the absolute number of Whites. The same is true in Canada. Soon, there will not be enough members of the majority to replace the majority-group baby boomers who are exiting the age of economic and civic activity.

Accordingly, we can expect the demographic transition to generate some degree of non-zero-sum mobility, even if its magnitude does not rival that of the post-World War II period. In the United States, we can already see important changes taking place at the top of the workforce, as the previous non-Hispanic White monopoly of these strata, where jobs often carry considerable authority, gives way to greater diversity (Alba and Yrizar Barbosa 2016). This shift is depicted in Table 2.1, which reports the percentage of non-Hispanic Whites who hold positions in the top quartile of the full-time workforce (the best remunerated occupations) by birth cohort and census year. The change is most apparent at the extremes. In the oldest cohort (56-65 year-olds) in 2000, almost 90 percent of top-quartile jobs were held by Whites, suggesting the degree of White monopoly until recent decades. However, reading Table 2.1 from right to left, we see that the White percentage declines with each new cohort and between 2000 and 2010. By the youngest cohort (26-35 year-olds) in 2010, the percentage has fallen to less than 70 percent. Since there is a close correspondence between the declining White percentage at the top of the workforce and the ethno-racial composition of each birth cohort, there is every reason to expect that the shift at the top will continue as the diversity of youthful labour force entrants grows.

Table 2.1. Growing Diversity at the Top of the Workforce: Non-Hispanic White Percentage of Top Occupational Quartile by Birth Cohort, United States, 2000 and 2010

	Pre-baby boom cohorts		Baby boom cohorts	
Year of birth	1975-84	1965-76	1945-65	1935-44
Age in 2000	—	26-35	36-45 46-55	56-65
Age in 2010	26-35	36-45	46-55 56-65	—
Percent in 2000	—	77.0	82.2 86.0	88.3
Percent in 2010	69.4	72.8	80.9 85.3	—

Source: Albas and Yrizar Barbosa (2016)

The data indicate, then, a widening entry into higher occupational tiers for non-Whites, as the number of Whites who can compete for positions declines. The groups that are benefitting most from this opening up at the top are of immigrant origin. In the United States, Black Americans, a category that includes some post-1965 immigrants and their children, have improved their representation in the top quartile but the gain has been small. The biggest changes involve Asians, both foreign- and U.S.-born, and U.S.-born Latinos. For instance, between the oldest working-age cohort in 2000 and the youngest in 2010, U.S.-born Hispanics went from 1.2 percent to 6.3 percent of top-quartile workers, a more than fivefold increase. The equivalent comparison for Asians shows a rise from 3.8 percent to 12.6 percent, a threefold increase.

Post-Great Recession data from the United States suggest that diversification at the top of the workforce has continued in the face of powerful economic headwinds. This observation does not deny that economic conditions have a pronounced impact on the magnitude of the updraft of non-White, immigrant-origin minorities. It merely recognizes that demography is powerful, too. Diversification will continue.

Mixed Unions and their Offspring

The most convincing evidence of the expansion of North American mainstreams comes from mixed unions and the accumulating evidence of the social locations of their offspring. As socioeconomic parity between Whites and some minorities rises and as demographic shifts also encourage higher rates of interaction between them, the level of mixed unions increases. This rise is evident in both Canada and the United States. In Canada, mixed unions now account for almost 4.6 percent of all married and cohabiting pairs. In the United States, where only marriages are closely tracked, intermarriages make up 8.4 percent of all marriages, rising to about 15 percent among the recently married (Frey 2015; Statistics Canada 2014; Wang 2012). In both countries also, the large majority of mixed unions unite a minority partner with a majority one—about 70 percent in the United States and 85 percent in Canada. The country differences—the higher rate of mixed unions in the United States, and the higher level of majority-minority unions in Canada—probably have more to do with the different ethno-racial compositions of their marriage-age populations than anything else (Hou et al. 2015). The percentage of non-White minorities is markedly higher south of the 49th parallel, increasing the frequency of White contacts with minorities.

In both countries, too, the rates of mixed-union formation by the second generations of major immigrant groups are robust, as Table 2.2 indicates.[2] (The second generation offers the proper test of mixing propensities because many in the first, or immigrant, generation are married when they arrive or, if single, lack the linguistic and cultural competencies to find partners outside their groups.) The great exception involves the children of Black immigrants in the United States. Visible African descent still carries heavy burdens in American society because of slavery and the institutional and cultural racism that arose in its wake (Alba and Foner, 2015). But apart from the low intermarriage frequency of

---

2. Editor's note: The Canadian data concern mixed marriages and cohabiting pairs, while the U.S. data concern mixed marriages only. Moreover, the Canadian data concern unions between Whites and members of minority groups plus unions between members of different minority groups, while the U.S. data concern only unions between members of minority groups and non-Hispanic Whites. Because of these differences, the Canadian and U.S. data are not strictly comparable, and conclusions from direct comparisons between the two sets of rates must be drawn cautiously.

Afro-Caribbeans, the rates for Asian and Latino second-generation groups are generally in the 25-45 percent range. (These are rates of intermarriage with non-Hispanic Whites. The rates would be higher if intermarriages with non-Whites were included.) Rates of mixed unions are even higher in Canada, commonly in the 50-75 percent range, although in this case mixed unions involving two minority partners are counted. Because the definitions behind the data are different, one cannot easily interpret the higher Canadian rates. They are possibly due to differences in ethno-racial composition in the marriage-age population, since smaller minority groups will have higher rates of mixing, all else the same (Hou et al. 2015). Another possible explanation is that Canada provides a more favourable context for second-generation mixing.

Table 2.2. Mixed Unions in the Second Generation by Group, Canada and the United States, in percent

Group (US if different)	Canada Men	Canada Women	United States Men	United States Women
Black (Afro-Caribbean)	71	56	12	9
Arab	50	42	na	na
South Asian (Indian)	37	38	27	21
Chinese	48	60	26	43
Filipino	62	71	35	43
Japanese	74	78	38	43
Korean	53	71	34	45
Southeast Asian (Vietnamese)	18	28	21	24
Latin American (Hispanic)	65	61	38	35

na = not available
Note: United States figures are for marriages with non-Hispanic Whites.
Sources: Alba and Foner (2015: 209); Canadian data thanks to Hélène Maheux of Statistics Canada.

By themselves, mixed unions constitute ambiguous evidence of mainstream expansion because it is not obvious whether intermarried couples are affiliated with the mainstream or with minority groups. Some ethnographic studies indicate that minority partners often face prejudice and cool toleration at best from the families of White partners (Song 2009). Less ambiguous is the accumulating data concerning the offspring of mixed unions, including partnerships without marriage. The social contexts in which these children grow up are diagnostic for the integrative character of mixed unions, as are their identity behaviour, social affiliations, and partner choices as adults. My evidence here comes from the United States, where two graduate students and I have been analyzing data about individuals from mixed family backgrounds (Alba et al. unpublished).

Individuals from mixed family backgrounds make up a substantial part of the child population in the United States. If we look at infants, who are more likely than older children to have two parents in the household, then 14-15 percent of those born in the United States have parents from two of the major ethno-racial categories. About three-quarters of them come from mixed majority-minority families. Many of these infants are invisible in conventional census data, where children are classified according to what their parents report about them. This is true in particular of the largest group, children who have one Hispanic parent and one non-Hispanic White parent; they constitute 40 percent of all infants of mixed background. Individuals who have both White and Black ancestry, often seen as the icon of ethno-racial mixing—represent about 10 percent of all these infants.

The social contexts in which these children grow up are one window into the integrative character of mixed unions. An examination of the income and residential characteristics of the families of mixed infants indicates that, on the whole, the families that mix one majority with one minority parent resemble all-White families more than they do the all-minority families that share the same minority origin. This situation is not just a matter of having characteristics like those of all-White families but also being located in similar residential locales and, by implication, having White families as neighbours. Families with a White mother and a Black father, which make up the great majority of White-Black unions, are the exception to these generalizations. The families that meld two minority origins look very much like other minority families.

If we examine the adult characteristics of individuals from mixed majority-minority family backgrounds—and, admittedly, the evidence is sparser here and must be evaluated more tentatively because of uncertainty about whether mixed backgrounds are fully reported—we again find a picture consistent with integration into the White mainstream for most individuals, with those of partly Black ancestry the prominent exception. In terms of social identities, the survey and census data seem consistent and supportive of the idea that for the most part these identities are more fluid and contingent than are the identities of individuals with ethno-racially unmixed backgrounds (Alba et al. unpublished; Lee and Bean 2010; Pew Research Center 2015). For individuals who are partly White but not Black, this fluidity often "tilts White" in the sense that they appear to incline more to the White side of their ancestry than to the minority side—importantly, in their sense of acceptance by others. For those who are partly Black, it tilts in the other direction.

A similar picture emerges from data about the social milieux of adults with these mixed backgrounds. When it comes to such interaction partners as friends and neighbours, most individuals from majority-minority backgrounds live in White-dominated worlds. For example, nearly half of those who are White and Asian say that most or all of their friends are Whites, compared to just 7 percent who say this about Asians. Near two-thirds say that all or most of their neighbors are Whites. Again, Black ancestry is an exception. Individuals who are White and Black are located in rather different contexts. Half of them say that all or most of their friends are Black.

And then there is marriage: Individuals who are partly White mostly take White partners. Miyawaki (2015) shows that White-American Indian and White-Asian individuals have high rates of marriage to Whites—around 70%. In this respect, Black ancestry is not so exceptional, for a majority of White/Black persons also marry Whites. In all cases, the rates of marriage to someone from their same minority background are much lower. Miyakawi's results are consistent with other analyses (Qian and Lichter 2011).

Conclusion

North American mainstreams appear to be opening up to allow entry by some non-European immigrants and their children, just as occurred historically with respect to Americans and Canadians having immigrant ancestors from less-favoured parts of Europe. This expansion is unlikely to have the sweep of the post-World War II mass assimilation of Jews and Catholics, who were mainly southern and eastern Europeans. The enormous rise in prosperity in North America in the quarter century or so following the war's end created non-zero-sum mobility on an unparalleled scale. The economic conditions of the early 21st century are more constraining. However, the ongoing demographic transition to diversity will also be associated with non-zero-sum mobility, and this impact is already visible in the upper tiers of the labour market. Thus, full entry to the mainstream, reflected in social integration with dominant Whites, will be a more selective process than in the past. Nevertheless, it will change the nature of the mainstream and thereby visibly alter both societies.

The historically high level of unions mixing Whites and non-Whites (Hispanics included) in Canada and the United States is having a pronounced impact on the population. In the United States, where mixed unions are more common than they are in Canada because of the greater percentage of minorities of marriageable age in the U.S. population, one of every seven infants has parents of different ethno-racial backgrounds, and the great majority of these infants come from mixed majority-minority families, where one parent is White and the other minority. Even when these unions are not permanent, their children will in the vast majority of cases grow up with networks of relatives who reflect the disparate backgrounds of their parents. This is a profoundly important development.

The social location of individuals of mixed background yields insights about the possible evolution of North American ethno-racial systems. However, much about them is hidden from view in the demographic data, which does not classify children according to their parents' backgrounds but on the basis of what parents say about them, which is often simplified. In the United States, individuals who are partly White and partly Hispanic are not even identifiable in demographic data because Hispanic ethnicity trumps race, and in many reports individuals with mixed racial backgrounds are classified as "minority" and not "White" (Alba 2016). Nevertheless, by exploiting what can be learned about the families of infants from census data and combining it with other sources of evidence, such as recent surveys and data on marriage patterns, we can assemble a reasonably consistent picture. Although the picture is only for the United States, there is no reason to believe that mixed backgrounds have a different social significance in Canada.

The picture indicates that a major impact of mixed unions involves an expansion of the mainstream, as neo-assimilation theory would lead one to believe. This is not to say that mixed unions are the only way that the mainstream may be expanding—many minority individuals in intermarriages with Whites and many upwardly mobile individuals in largely White work and residential contexts are also joining the mainstream. But the children of mixed minority-majority unions offer convincing evidence of mainstream expansion. These children are generally being raised in families with incomes close to or above the average for children in White families, and they are located in the kinds of residential spaces where White families also are concentrated. A variety of evidence demonstrates that, when they grow up, their ethno-racial identities are unusually fluid and contingent. For individuals who are part White and part American Indian, Asian, or Hispanic, those identities tilt White in the sense that these individuals more readily declare themselves to be White than minority and feel a sense of affinity with Whites. They do not generally perceive racial barriers to their participation in mainstream settings. They tend to live in neighbourhoods with many White neighbors and they have high rates of marriage to Whites.

The exceptions to these patterns are individuals who are White and Black. On average, they grow up in families that are less affluent than other children in majority-minority families. Their identities tilt Black and they report discriminatory experiences—with the police, for example—that are consonant with their being treated as minority group members. Nevertheless, they also sometimes identify as Whites, and they have rates of marriage to Whites that are far higher than the general Black-White intermarriage rate. The evidence about individuals of mixed, all-minority origins is scanty but is consistent with their treatment as minority group members.

We can gain additional insight into this hypothesized expansion of the mainstream by recalling some of the features of the post-

World War II mass assimilation of so-called White ethnics. Then, as now, assimilation did not require wholesale conformity to a White Protestant model. The assimilating ethnics, who were for the most part not Protestant, did not in most cases convert to the religion of the majority. During their assimilation, they continued to claim some degree of ethnic distinctiveness, to the extent that many observers in both Canada and the United States thought they were seeing an ethnic revival (Jacobson 2006). However, in retrospect, "symbolic ethnicity," with its muted identities and ethnic claims, consistent with embeddedness in ethnically mixed social milieux, is the more appropriate conceptual fit (Gans 1979).

These same features likely apply to the current expansion, indicating another wave of diversification within the mainstream (Vasquez 2014). This will mean, for example, that many mainstream individuals of recent immigrant origin will continue to assert identities derived from these backgrounds, including mixed identities, and to employ cultural features associated with their origins to distinguish themselves from mainstream Whites. But if this mainstream diversification resembles that of the White ethnics, as seems plausible, these ethno-cultural assertions will have a symbolic character, meaning that they will be muted and will not interfere with social interactions in mainstream settings, which involve others who are White or who do not share the same minority origins.

This diversification is not just affecting the mainstream, but also the minority populations, at least as conventionally measured. Many individuals of mixed or minority background who are gaining entry into mainstream contexts continue to identify, at least some of the time, with their minority origin. However, their social characteristics, such as their occupation, residential location and cultural background, differ from those of others with the same minority origin. Mainstream expansion therefore underscores the growing heterogeneity of minority groups.

To point to the previous period of assimilation is in no way to claim that history is repeating itself. The macro-economic context for mass assimilation is much less favourable today. The quarter century following World War II was a period of unusually high prosperity, featuring a low level of economic inequality and a major expansion of post-secondary education and of middle-class occupations. In addition, a low level of undocumented status among immigrant parents did not create a drag on the second generation. These characteristics created an unusually favourable context for mobility by ethnic minorities without intensification of competition along ethnic lines (Alba 2009). Today, economic inequality is high and socioeconomic mobility is stunted; levels of undocumented status are at an historical peak. Indicators of assimilation achieved much higher values in the earlier period (Alba and Nee 2003).

Nevertheless, the current analysis has demonstrated that assimilation is still an important force in Canada and the United States and must be taken into account in understanding how the ethno-racial systems of these two countries might be influenced by mass immigration since 1965. This is not the assimilation of the post-World War II period, which reshaped racial boundaries by expanding the White population; it is more individually selective. But now as then, the mainstream is expanding and also becoming more diverse, this time by including more individuals who do not identify exclusively as Whites.

References

Alba, R. 2009. *Blurring the Color Line: The New Chance for a More Integrated America.* Cambridge: Harvard University Press.

_____. 2016. "The Likely Persistence of a White Majority: How Census Bureau Statistics Have Misled Thinking about the American Future." *The American Prospect* 27(1): 67-71.

Alba, R., B. Beck, and D. Basaran Sahin. Unpublished. "The U.S. mainstream expands—again." Department of Sociology, CUNY Graduate Center.

Alba, R. and N. Foner. 2015. *Strangers No More: Immigration and the Challenges of Integration in North America and Western Europe.* Princeton: Princeton University Press.

Alba, R. and V. Nee. 2003. *Remaking the American Mainstream: Assimilation and Contemporary Immigration.* Cambridge: Harvard University Press, 2003.

Alba, R., A. Raboteau, and J. DeWind. 2009. *Immigration and Religion in America: Comparative and Historical Perspectives.* New York: NYU Press.

Alba, R., J. Reitz, and P. Simon. 2012. "National Conceptions of Assimilation, Integration and Cohesion." Pp. 44-63 in *The Changing Face of World Cities: Young Children of Immigrants in Europe and the United States,* M. Crul and J. Mollenkopf, eds. New York: Russell Sage Foundation.

Alba, R. and G. Yrizar Barbosa. 2016. "Room at the Top? Minority Mobility and the Transition to Demographic Diversity in the U.S." *Ethnic and Racial Studies* 39(4): 917-38.

Baltzell, E. D. 1964. *The Protestant Establishment: Aristocracy and Caste in America.* New York: Random House.

Bean, F., S. Brown, and J. Bachmeier. 2015. *Parents without Papers: The Progress and Pitfalls of Mexican-American Integration.* New York: Russell Sage Foundation.

Bloemraad, I. 2006. *Becoming a Citizen: Incorporating Immigrants and Refugees in the United States and Canada.* Berkeley: University of California Press.

Corak, M. 2013. "Income Inequality, Equality of Opportunity, and Intergenerational Mobility." *Journal of Economic Perspectives* 27(3): 79-102.

Fishman, S. B. 2004. *Double or Nothing: Jewish Families and Mixed Marriage.* Waltham MA: Brandeis University Press.

Frey, W. 2015. *The Diversity Explosion: How New Racial Demographics Are Remaking America.* Washington DC: The Brookings Institution.

Gans, H. 1979. "Symbolic Ethnicity: The Future of Ethnic Groups and Cultures in America." *Ethnic and Racial Studies* 2(1): 1-20.

Gerstle, G. 2001. *American Crucible: Race and Nation in the Twentieth Century.* Princeton: Princeton University Press.

Gordon, M 1964. *Assimilation in American Life.* New York: Oxford University Press.

Hou, F., Z. Wu, C. Schimmele, and J. Myles. 2015. "Cross-Country Variation in Interracial Marriage: A USA-Canada Comparison of Metropolitan Areas." *Ethnic and Racial Studies* 38(9): 1591-1609.

Jacobson, M. F. 2006. *Roots Too: White Ethnic Revival in Post-Civil Rights America.* Cambridge MA: Harvard University Press.

Kymlicka, W. 2010. "The Current State of Multiculturalism in Canada and Research Themes on Canadian Multiculturalism 2008-2010." Report to the Department of Citizenship and Integration Canada.

Lee, J. and F. Bean. 2010. *The Diversity Paradox: Immigration and the Color Line in Twenty-First Century America.* New York: Russell Sage Foundation.

Li, P. 2003. "Deconstructing Canada's Discourse of Immigrant Integration." *Journal of International Migration and Integration* 4(3): 315-33.

Miyawaki, M. 2015. "Expanding Boundaries of Whiteness? A Look at the Marital Patterns of Part-White Multiracial Groups." *Sociological Forum* 30(4): 995-1016.

Ngai, M. 2003. *Impossible Subjects: Illegal Aliens and the Making of Modern America.* Princeton: Princeton University Press.

Pew Research Center. 2015. *Multiracial in America: Proud, Diverse and Growing in Numbers.* Washington D.C.

Perlmann, J. 2005. *Italians Then, Mexicans Now: Immigrant Origins and Second-Generation Progress, 1890-2000*. New York: Russell Sage Foundation.

Porter, J. 1965. *The Vertical Mosaic: An Analysis of Social Class and Power in Canada*. Toronto: University of Toronto Press.

Qian, Z. and D. Lichter. 2011. "Changing Patterns of Interracial Marriage in a Multiracial Society." *Journal of Marriage and Family* 73(5): 1065-84.

Song, M. 2009. "Is Intermarriage a Good Indicator of Integration?" *Journal of Ethnic and Migration Studies* 35(2): 331-48.

Statistics Canada. 2010. "Projections of the Diversity of the Canadian Population: 2006 to 2031." http://www.statcan.gc.ca/pub/91-551-x/91-551-x2010001-eng.pdf.

_____. 2014. "Mixed Unions in Canada." http://www12.statcan.gc.ca/nhs-enm/2011/as-sa/99-010-x/99-010-x2011003_3-eng.pdf.

Vasquez, J. 2014. "The Whitening Hypothesis Challenged: Biculturalism in Latino and Non-Hispanic White Intermarriage." *Sociological Forum* 29(2): 386-407.

Wang, W. 2012. "The Rise of Intermarriage: Rates, Characteristics Vary by Race and Gender." Pew Research Center. https://www.supremecourt.gov/opinions/URLs_Cited/OT2015/14-981/14-981-10.pdf.

Wertheimer, J. and S. M. Cohen. 2014. "The Pew Survey Reanalyzed: More Bad News, but a Glimmer of Hope." *Mosaic: Advancing Jewish Thought*. http://mosaicmagazine.com/essay/2014/11/the-pew-survey-reanalyzed/.

CHAPTER THREE

Multicultural Nation-building and Canada's Future: Implications of Comparative Research

Jeffrey G. Reitz

Canadian Exceptionalism?
Global migration is occurring on an unprecedented scale, representing a grand mixing of the world's peoples, with profound implications for the fate of nations and for humanity as a whole. The Canadian experience with global migration appears to be one of the most positive. The proportion of foreign-born residents in Canada is among the highest of the major industrial countries (United Nations 2013). Nevertheless, Canadians are least likely to say we have too many immigrants, and we are most likely to see immigration as an opportunity rather than a problem (German Marshall Fund 2010). Our commitment to immigration has weathered the spread of international terrorism, the rise of xenophobic racism, and the increasingly pervasive employment difficulties of immigrants.

To see how contemporary trends in Canada may unfold, we must consider the reasons for "Canadian exceptionalism" on immigration. What is the basis for our positive stance toward immigration? Many people point to our reputation for tolerance and inclusiveness, or our multicultural policies and traditions. These are likely important factors. But what are the underlying reasons for these characteristics, the forces that have reinforced their salience now and are likely to shape future trends?

For much of our history, Canada's attitude to immigration was similar to that of other "settler societies" like the United States and Australia. We strongly preferred immigrants of European background, especially northern European background, and disdained others. Our engagement with "multiculturalism" was prompted by special circumstances related to Canada's French-English duality. Quebec's "Quiet Revolution" initiated a debate over bilingualism and biculturalism, and replacing biculturalism with multiculturalism emerged as a key to resolving the tension between the demands of the Québécois and those of immigrant groups. Prime Minister Pierre Trudeau's multiculturalism policy increased immigrant support for bilingualism and may also have helped maintain French-Canadian support for immigration.

The negotiations leading to the adoption of Canada's multiculturalism policy do not necessarily help explain our relative success in immigrant integration. To understand Canada's distinctiveness in this regard, we must compare Canada with other countries. When we do that, we find that our positive experience with immigration has economic reasons that are related to our policy of selecting highly educated immigrants.

An important point of comparison is the United States. While many Americans embrace diversity and inclusiveness, the United States has not adopted a policy like Canada's multiculturalism policy, and immigration debates in the United States have grown increasingly contentious in recent years. However, lack of a multiculturalism policy in the United States hardly explains its immigration controversy. Instead, the difficulties of American experience with diversity derive in large measure from two inescapable circumstances that do not affect Canada: the legacy of slavery and the border with Mexico. Their impact on diversity issues in the United States is enormous. Thus, the successful presidential campaign of Donald Trump generated a racist discourse directed at many targets but mainly at Blacks and Mexicans. Trump declared his intention to build a wall on the Mexican border, an idea that many Canadians deplore. Yet we do not experience the type of uncontrolled migration that concerns Americans. As *The Economist* (2016) put it with reference to Canadian immigration: "It is easier to be relaxed about immigration when your only land border is protected by a wall the size of the United States." In other words, by virtue of geography we have what the United States and many other countries want: control over immigration.

If we set aside the two American problems related to the history of slavery and contemporary undocumented immigration from Mexico, and focus on comparable immigration steams from Asia, the Caribbean, and Africa, we find that the United States looks much like Canada. In both countries, immigrants from the latter regions are highly educated, they have jobs that are about as good in relation to education as their counterparts in Canada have, and their children attain high levels of education and do just as well as in Canada. Their general experience integrating in the two countries is much the same (Reitz 2014; Attewell, Kasinitz, and Dunn 2010). It follows that celebrating multiculturalism as the cause of major differences may be misguided.

Immigration increasingly affects all industrial countries, and the comparison of Canadian immigration experience with what has happened in Europe is increasingly relevant for Canadians. Trends in Europe clearly have been relatively negative, with a rise in xenophobic politics and increasing Islamophobia. The United Kingdom and the Netherlands have unceremoniously scrapped their experiments with multiculturalism policy, something not even remotely considered in Canada. Again, however, the circumstances shaping immigration experiences in Europe are different from those in Canada.

Much contemporary immigration in Europe is post-colonial: migration from former colonies to the metropole, often unregulated and not necessarily in tune with contemporary national priorities. Comparison of public opinion shows dramatic differences in public perceptions related to the economics of immigration. Whereas in Canada more than 60 percent of the population agrees that "immigrants are generally good for the country's economy," in most European countries a majority believes the opposite (ISSP National Identity Survey 2003). Why? In Canada, selection of immigrants strongly emphasizes their positive economic impact. In Europe, relatively unregulated immigration lies behind some of the most negative attitudes of the public. The *independent* impact of differences in openness to cultural diversity on receptivity to immigrants has not been demonstrated empirically.

In the comparative analysis of immigrant integration, analysts have focused on national models for immigrant reception—multiculturalism in Canada and more assimilationist approaches in the United States and France, for example. The effort to assess whether multiculturalism has a positive effect on immigrant integration has prompted the creation of a Multiculturalism Policy Index that ranks countries according to the robustness of this type of policy (Kymlicka 2012: 7). Analyses employing this index have debunked the idea that these policies have much of an influence on immigrant integration (van Reekum, Duyvendak, and Bertossi 2012; Torrekens and Jacobs 2016). The effort to include a wider range of policies in the mix resulted in the creation of the Migrant Integration Policy Index (2015), but it has not been directly related to immigrant integration outcomes.

The most extensive review of comparative data on immigrant integration compares the United States and Canada with the United Kingdom, France, Germany, and the Netherlands (Alba and Foner 2015). It notes that a focus on "national models" is one of a series of "grand narratives" in debates about immigrant integration. Other such narratives include the effects of the political economy of the labour market and the welfare state; whether the receiving countries are settler societies like Canada and the United States; and the effect of nation-specific factors like the history of slavery in the United States. They find the North American and European countries little different on immigrant integration. Strengths in one area are typically offset by weakness in another. For example, Canada and the United States offer immigrants more opportunity because of their relatively unregulated labour markets, but those labour markets are more unequal than those in the European countries, creating obstacles for immigrants. While race is a bigger barrier in Canada and the United States, religion is more important in the United Kingdom, France, Germany, and the Netherlands. Alba and Foner (2015: 231) conclude that while national models "are not irrelevant," no case is especially distinctive.

The case of France is of particular interest for Canada because the two "national models" are almost opposite to one another. Anti-immigrant sentiment in France is characterized by its bans on Muslim dress for women, civil unrest in Muslim neighborhoods, and the rise of the National Front led by Marine Le Pen, which advocates a moratorium on legal migration and an end to regularization of illegal immigrants. The French discourse on immigration references republican values, maintaining colour-blind policies, and excluding ethnic markers from the civic arena. It seems to be the opposite of Canadian multiculturalism. One instance is the enforcement of public secularism (*laïcité*), which has apparently important consequences for the Muslim population with its relatively public expressions of religion (Bowen 2007).

Is Canada more successful at integrating immigrants than France, specifically in the case of Muslims? In the following, I summarize preliminary and emerging results from my current research, which focuses on this question. Generally, my conclusions fit with those of Alba and Foner (2015). If differences exist, they are small. However, my research adds two features to their review.

One additional feature of my research is to distinguish the province of Québec within Canada. This is not always done in cross-national comparisons, but it is essential because the "national model" in Québec is somewhat different from that in the rest of Canada, particularly where multiculturalism is at issue, and this difference is important in any comparison with France. While Québec is a nation of immigrants like the rest of Canada, 78 percent of its population has French as a mother tongue, and its enthusiasm for multiculturalism is dampened considerably by the fact that adoption of multiculturalism in Canada in some ways downgraded concerns about French cultural survival within the country. Recently, Québec's discourse on immigration has reflected thinking in France, and its policies of immigrant integration may be seen as standing somewhere between the rest of Canada and France. For example, Québec's debates, like those in France, have focused on religious minorities, and the debate over "reasonable accommodation" of difference reflected French influence. Québec's proposed Charter of Values seemed so French it was endorsed by French President François Hollande. Instead of multiculturalism, Québec pursues *interculturalisme*, espousing pluralism but allowing the provincial government to promote mainstream French culture (Banting and Soroka 2012).

The second feature of my study that adds to Alba and Foner's work is that I frame comparisons to take account of the distinctive composition of Canada's immigrant groups, including Muslims. Before differences in immigrant experience may be attributed to context, it is necessary to take account of the impact of differences in the characteristics of immigrant groups themselves. This is no trivial issue. Alba and Foner focus on "low status" immigrants, by which they mean stigmatized minorities with low levels of education, like Mexicans in the United States. Muslims in France, mostly from North Africa, qualify as low status immigrants since half have high school education or less. Comparing France and Canada is not straightforward because our visible minority immigrants may be stigmatized to an extent, but they are not low status in the Alba/Foner sense because they are generally highly educated. In Canada, one third of Muslims have bachelor's degrees, and fewer than 20 percent have high school or less, whereas in France, as many as half have high school education or less.

In addition, Canadian Muslims are different in origins and more diverse than their counterparts in France. They come from Pakistan and countries across the Middle East and Africa, whereas French Muslims are mainly from North Africa. Canadian Muslims are proportionately less numerous too, constituting 3 percent of population compared to 7-8 percent in France, and they are on average more recent arrivals. The effect of all these differences must be considered in an analysis of immigrant integration.

My research includes several data sources, quantitative and qualitative. National surveys of ethnic diversity are exceedingly important in my analysis. The French "Trajectories and Origins" survey was conducted in 2008 (Beauchemin, Hamel, and Simon 2015). It provides extensive data on ethnic groups and second generation minorities. The French survey is comparable in design and scale to the Canadian "Ethnic Diversity Survey" of 2002 (Statistics Canada 2003).

Do Public Attitudes Match the National Models?

Our first finding concerns public attitudes, based on data sources such as the World Values Survey and the International Social Survey Program. Interestingly, public attitudes do not always match the themes of political and media discourse. We tapped two dimensions of multicultural values. The first concerns respondents' views on the extent to which immigrants can become full members of a national society. They were asked if they agree or disagree with a statement about whether it is possible for minority cultural groups to become full members of society. The second dimension concerns openness to cultural diversity. Respondents were asked if they think it is better for ethnic and racial groups to "maintain their distinct customs and traditions" or "adapt and blend into the larger society." In Figure 3.1, we have located each of several countries on these two dimensions, plotted on the vertical and horizontal dimensions, respectively.

The upper right quadrant represents the most multicultural val-

Figure 3.1. National Values of Immigrant Inclusion and Exclusion

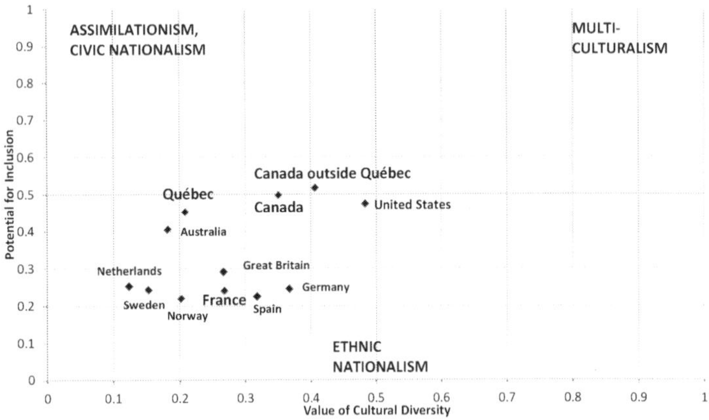

[Scatter plot with vertical axis "Potential for Inclusion" (0 to 1) and horizontal axis "Value of Cultural Diversity" (0 to 1). Upper left quadrant labelled "ASSIMILATIONISM, CIVIC NATIONALISM"; upper right labelled "MULTICULTURALISM"; lower right labelled "ETHNIC NATIONALISM". Data points: Québec, Canada, Canada outside Québec, United States, Australia, Netherlands, Great Britain, Germany, Sweden, France, Norway, Spain.]

Source: International Social Survey Programme: National Identity II - ISSP (2003).

ues. The attitudes of Canadians outside Quebec are similar to those of Americans. French attitudes, while less multicultural, are in the same range as those in the United Kingdom and the Netherlands, both of which have flirted with multiculturalist policies. Québec is a settler society but more assimilationist than France is.

France is more secular than the Anglo-Saxon countries, as shown in responses to questions regarding the desirability of churches speaking out on abortion and homosexuality, and Quebeckers are moving in the direction of France. These similarities are a product of history, and especially of the fact that the Church was a target in the French Revolution and Québec's Quiet Revolution.

Much data demonstrate that the overall attitudes of Quebeckers to immigration are similar to the attitudes of Canadians outside Québec. Quebeckers are as favourable to immigration as Canadians are elsewhere, while the French follow the pattern across Europe and in the United States, with majorities in favour of reductions in immigration. Quebeckers are also more like Canadians outside Québec in seeing the economic and cultural value of immigration. The relatively favourable attitudes to immigration in Canada including Québec compared to France is explained more by differences in perceptions of the economic value of immigration than by attitudes toward multicultural values or secularism. This conclusion is based on a cross-national regression analysis of attitudinal data, summarized in Figure 3.2. The "baseline" bars indicate

**Figure 3.2.
Regression of Preference for More Immigrants on Predictors**

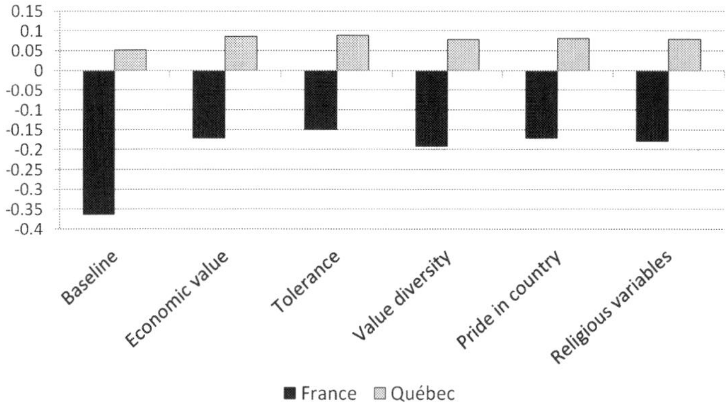

■ France □ Québec

Source: International Social Survey Programme: National Identity II - ISSP (2003).

support for immigration in France (Black) and among Quebeckers (grey), both as compared to Canadians outside Québec. Moving from left to right, we see, first, that compared to Canadians outside Québec, the French are considerably more opposed to immigration. Perhaps surprisingly, Quebeckers are slightly more in favour of immigration compared to Canadians outside Québec. Second, when we control for perceptions of the economic value of immigration, differences across settings are reduced substantially, showing the importance of this factor. Adding more value items to the regression equation has little effect on attitudes toward immigration in either Québec or France.

Thus, the distinctive Canadian receptivity to immigration compared to France is shown to be significantly driven by perceptions of the underlying economics, not the values debated so prominently in public discourse. If you think something bears a high cost, you may be open to arguments about why it is bad. If you think something is enriching you, you may be open to arguments about why it is good. Negative discourse on immigration resulting from worries about immigrants as an economic burden may make the French look worse than they are. The more positive discourse in Canada, including Quebec, results from beliefs that university-educated immigrants are an economic asset, perhaps making us look "nicer" than we really are.

Social Inclusion and Exclusion: Social Realities behind the Immigration Debates

To help us understand Canada's comparative success with immigration, I now provide an overview of the experiences of Muslim and other immigrants in France and Canada. Where possible, I distinguish Québec from the rest of Canada. I examine social, economic, and political dimensions of integration. National survey and census-based data help us to go beyond anecdotal media accounts by comparing experiences across large, representative samples or entire populations. To focus on the impact of religion, I compare Muslims to other immigrant minorities (meaning immigrants and the second generation).

Regarding social integration, various indicators are available from nationally representative surveys. Based on a comparison of the 2008 "Trajectories and Origins" survey in France (about 21,000 interviews) and the 2002 "Ethnic Diversity Survey" in Canada (about 42,000 interviews), our analysis (Reitz, Simon, and Laxer forthcoming) show broad similarities in obstacles to Muslim social integration in the larger society. A significant Muslim/non-Muslim gap in social inclusion exists in all three settings. It results more from ethnic, cultural, and racial differences than from religious differences. Here I review two indicators, reports of discrimination and national identification and their implications.

Muslims in France and Canada more often report discrimination than do non-Muslim minorities and to about the same degree—roughly 35 percent of Muslims compared to about 20-25 percent of non-Muslim minorities. Within Canada there is no significant difference between Québec and the rest of the country. Generational status matters: second generation Muslims in France and Canada report discrimination much more often than do first generation immigrants.

The geographical origins of Muslims and other minorities differ in France and Canada. However, visible minority status appears to be behind much of the Muslim discrimination in both countries. Figure 3.3 shows that only about 12 percent of European-origin groups in France and Canada report discrimination. For all non-European groups, Muslim and otherwise, the figures are about three times higher. Beyond this finding, religion matters somewhat more in France, and race somewhat more in Canada. Looking at Muslims, we see that those from the Maghreb and Sub-Saharan Africa in France somewhat more often report discrimination than do Muslims of Middle East and South Asian origin in Canada.

To clearly see the effect of religion on discrimination we must compare people of the same geographical origin. France has Muslims and non-Muslims from the Maghreb and sub-Saharan Africa,

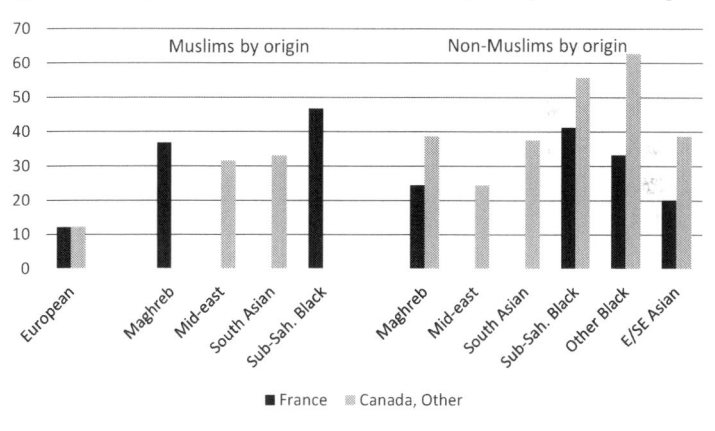

Figure 3.3. Experience of Discrimination by Religion and Origin

Source: France: Trajectories and Origins Survey (2009); Canada: Ethnic Diversity Survey (2002).

and in both cases, Muslim status slightly boosts reports of discrimination. In Canada, Muslim status boosts reports of discrimination for those from the Middle East but lowers it for South Asians. Muslim status seems to matter a bit more in France. Race matters more in Canada, since for Blacks who are non-Muslim, both sub-Saharan and "other" (mainly Caribbean), reports of discrimination are much more frequent in Canada than in France. This is also true for East and Southeast Asian minorities.

I conclude that, while Muslim status is somewhat more strongly associated with perception of discrimination in France than in Canada, and race is somewhat more strongly associated with perception of discrimination in Canada than in France, race matters more than religion in both settings. This conclusion is supported by two other findings. First, respondents themselves say it. Only about one-third of French and Canadian Muslims who reported discrimination said it was based on religion; most Muslims mentioned race, skin colour, national origins, or accent. Second, Muslims who are more religious do not report more frequent discrimination than Muslims who are less religious. In fact, the effect of greater religiosity is *less* for Muslims than for other religious groups.

The socio-demographic composition of Muslim and minorities differ in France and Canada. On average, French Muslims are longer-established and Canadian Muslims have higher levels of education. A detailed cross-national comparison shows that the two factors are somewhat offsetting and do not materially affect my overall conclusions. The higher average level of education of Canadian Muslims boosts reports of discrimination; their more recent arrival dampens it.

Another indicator of significance in assessing social integration is national identification. This variable is more difficult to measure and was measured differently in each setting. In France, people were asked about their level of agreement with the statement, "I feel French." In Canada, the question was about ethnic identity, with Canadian identity indicated by including "Canadian" as one response. The difference is perhaps inevitable; certainly one could not use the term "ethnic" in France, and in Québec we do not have an uncontested national identity. Nonetheless, we can examine the Muslim/non-Muslim difference and compare across settings.

We find that Muslims identify nationally in France and Canada less often than do other minorities. The effects of generation are about the same in both countries. For Québec, there is an important difference because of the contested mainstream identity. Our measure of mainstream identification includes "Canadian," "Canadien" and "Québécois." Mainstream francophones tend to consider themselves "Québecois" while Anglophones tend to choose "Canadian." Other minority group members more often choose "Canadian" than "Québécois," so in a sense they are adopting an identity of the national mainstream, not the Québec mainstream. This is an effect of the subnational status of Québec rather than the French cultural connection. In this respect, the issue of minority identity is different in Québec and France. The similar assimilationist impulse has different roots.

Regarding national identity we can examine not only "feeling French" and "feeling Canadian" but also feeling *accepted* as French or Canadian. A question in the French survey asked respondents their level of agreement with the statement, "People see me as French." Forty to 45 percent of all non-European minorities who were citizens disagreed and did *not* think people saw them as French. The percentages were about the same for Muslims and non-Muslims. There was a substantial difference for racial groups. Only 10 percent of European-origin minority group members did not see themselves as French.

The strong national identity of French Muslims combined with the emotional impact of not feeling accepted as French is clearly illustrated in a case study of a group of women in Paris protesting a headscarf ban imposed on mothers wanting to participate in school activities (Kassir and Reitz, 2016). Our interviews with the mothers showed that although headscarf bans ostensibly are there to oppose stereotypical Muslim traditions of public religion and the submissive woman, the protest did not defend either of these points. Instead, it took the form of a feminist movement. The protesters felt it was the right of mothers *as French women* to participate in school activities. To protest, the women had to move a certain distance from the Muslim men who did not support them, imams in particular. One woman said: "It is our human right that they violated and now I will not wait for a pope or a priest or whoever to tell me if I can fight or not."

In Canada there is the roughly parallel case of Zunera Ishaq, who protested when she was denied citizenship based on a policy put in place by Prime Minister Harper that forbade wearing the *niqab* to the citizenship ceremony. She subsequently published an opinion piece in the *Toronto Star* arguing from a feminist position. Using words similar to those of the French mothers, she said: "I am not looking for Mr. Harper to approve my life choices or dress. I am certainly not looking for him to speak on my behalf and 'save' me from oppression" (Ishaq 2015).

We have another source for gauging the emotional impact of minority-group feelings of acceptance and rejection: national health surveys, which tap standard indicators of psychological distress and can be used to compare Muslim and non-Muslim minorities. These are the 2001-02 Canadian Community Health Survey (Béland 2002) and the 2008 French *Enquête Santé sur la Protection Sociale* (Allonier, Douirgnon, and Rochereau 2010). A battery of questions in French and Canadian surveys ask, for example, how often respondents felt "tired out for no reason," "sad," "nervous," or "down in the dumps." Although the scales are somewhat different in the French and Canadian surveys, the results can be standardized to an international norm (Joly and Reitz 2015). Psychological distress is a significant component of social integration and may reflect the resilience of immigrants as they address problems of integration more generally.

We found that, on average, Muslim minority-group members experience a higher level of psychological distress than do members of other minority groups in English Canada as well as in France. In Québec, though the sample is small, we find that Muslim minority-group members experience a lower level of psychological distress than do members of other minority groups. The Muslim/non-Muslim difference is not related to the strength of religious attachment but is associated with unemployment and labour market inactivity. These findings reinforce the view that the effect of Muslim status on social integration is not hugely different in France and Canada, and may be smaller still in Québec. The issue of minority religion so salient in the media seems to be a much weaker factor "on the ground."

Economic Integration: Differences of Labour Market Structure and Headscarf Bans

When we turn to employment and earnings, we start to find the most significant differences across settings. To that end, let us examine the individual-equivalent household incomes of Muslims relative to other minorities of non-European origin in Canada (using 2001 census data) and France (the "Trajectories and Origins" survey). ("Individual-equivalent" household income measures the economic well-being of individuals by adjusting household incomes according to household size and ages of members.) In brief, Muslims in France and Canada, including Québec, earn about two-thirds as much as members of non-Muslim, non-European immigrant groups. To some extent, this figure masks differences in opportunity structures, which may be more readily visible when we compare the standing of relatively recently-arrived Muslim immigrants with those who have arrived earlier and those who were native-born.

Analysis shows that, while recent immigrants in Canada, including those in Québec, experience more economic hardship than do their counterparts in France, those residing in the country longer and those born in Canada do better. Analysis also suggests that some of this difference is a result of the educational profiles of minorities in the two countries and the larger proportion of the native-born generation who acquire a university education in Canada. However, the second generation in France does acquire significantly more education than do immigrant parents, and the difference in mobility patterns is observed for minorities regardless of level of education. A more important cause is the difference in labour market regimes. The more regulated labour environment in France provides more adequate initial income for Muslims in France; a relatively open and fluid labour market, as in Canada, provides increased opportunity over time.

A comparison of individual-equivalent household incomes (not shown here) demonstrates that Muslim disadvantage is greater in France than in Canada. However, when we take account of origins, education, place of residence, time of arrival, and generation, things even out, with little difference between France, Québec and the rest of Canada. The lower economic position of Muslims in France is caused mainly by lower levels of immigrant education and a more rigid labour market in that country. The visible concentration of Muslims in low-income areas is a result of these factors plus their large numbers, not a difference in the effect of Muslim status itself.

A significant difference between settings also emerges when we examine the status of women in the labour market. In Canada, analysis of 2001 census data shows that fewer than 50 percent of recent immigrant Muslim women are in the labour force (Reitz, Phan, and Banerjee 2015). The percentage is about the same for Hindus and Sikhs but varies by region of origin. A pattern of assimilation exists for groups with longer residence in Canada and for the Muslim second generation. The gender difference in labour market participation converges with that of the mainstream groups, represented by native-born Whites who are either Christian or have no religious affiliation.

For France, the same pattern of assimilation of Muslim women into the labour market exists with one exception: assimilation is less complete for the second generation. For Muslim women born in France, the gender gap in labour force participation is about 15 percent greater than is the case the mainstream labour force, whereas there is virtually no such gap in Canada.

Public policies and attitudes against the wearing of a headscarf by Muslim women are stronger in France but have by no means eliminated the practice. My analysis of "Trajectories and Origins" survey data shows that among Muslim women in France, about 20 percent of immigrants always wear a headscarf in public, regardless of how long they have lived in the country, and as many as 10 percent of those born in France always do so. Wearing a headscarf in France today carries significant implications for employment opportunity. Our qualitative interviews suggest that many young women in France wear the headscarf as a political protest or as part of generational rebellion. They are often defying the opinions of their parents who want them to be successful in employment. But generational rebellion means the assimilationist headscarf policy backfires.

Interestingly, relatively low labour force participation of Muslim women in France does not affect household income. This fact may be the outcome of state income support. If so, the implication is ironic: French taxpayers are subsidizing the exclusion of Muslim women resulting from the headscarf ban.

Political Integration: Offsetting Differences in Citizenship and Voting

Analysis of survey data in a recent paper shows that immigrants in Canada, including Muslims, become citizens faster than do their French counterparts (Laxer and Reitz 2016). At the same time, voter participation rates for those who are citizens are about the same in France, Québec, and the rest of Canada. The "ethnic vote" is more often discussed in Canada than in France but in both countries members of minority groups vote in considerable number and thus have an impact on politics.

Alba and Foner (2015) compared France and Canada on the representation of immigrants in public office. They found such representation higher in Canada at the federal level but lower at the regional and municipal level. Immigrants who are not citizens are eligible to vote in French municipal elections, and political parties have a role in selecting candidates for municipal office. It appears that these differences matter. During the period 2001-12, the mayor of Paris was Tunisian-born Bertrand Delanoë, a man of mixed French and Tunisian background. He was controversial less for being Tunisian than for being gay. In the 2014 elections, he was replaced by Anne Hidalgo, who is Spanish and born in Spain. In Canada, such elections would be celebrated as victories for multiculturalism. In France, these facts were largely ignored.

Implications for Canada: Remembering the Economic Bases of Multiculturalism

While public discourses on immigration in France, Québec, and English Canada reflect real differences in social values related to multiculturalism and religion, these differences are not as great as they seem. Moreover, they are not primary determinants of differences in public attitudes to immigration. Such differences depend more on the characteristics of the immigrants arriving in each place. We can celebrate multiculturalism but we should also remember that people in countries where immigration is controversial often only want what Canadians take for granted: control over immigration. Control over immigration helps ensure its positive economic contribution.

If we see public rhetoric on multiculturalism in Canada, and republicanism and secularism in France, as reflecting not the social roots of national differences in attitudes to immigration, but to some extent as *rationalizations* for these attitudes, dressed up by reference to symbols linked to national ideals or patriotic obligations, then we can appreciate the limited impact they have on the experience of immigrants. Our findings comparing Muslims in France, Québec and the rest of Canada indicate that Muslims experience significant barriers to integration in all three settings, and that these barriers are based not so much on religion as on race or cultural origins, which affect non-Muslim minority groups too. The highly visible economic struggles of Muslim minorities in the *banlieues* of France, compared to the more buoyant situation of Muslims in Québec and the rest of Canada, occur not so much because Muslims receive more negative treatment in France compared to the treatment of non-Muslim groups. Rather, they result from the relatively low level of education of Muslim immigrants in France, their large numbers, and the rigidities of the French labour market. There are important differences in policies affecting Muslim immigrants, such as more restrictive citizenship law and headscarf bans in France, and these definitely are part of the difficulties faced by Muslims there. However, in comparative context, the impact of these policies is offset to some degree by other factors, such as greater representation of minority groups in municipal politics and relatively generous income support for families.

Seeing differences in public discourse as partly derivative of underlying economic factors also helps explain the somewhat conflicted situation in Québec. Québec's anti-immigrant discourse borrows from France but ultimately French policies have not been adopted in Québec. That is because of the basically positive attitudes in Québec to immigration and the perception of the high economic value of immigrants. It may also be to some degree because, while it may be more difficult to link pro-immigrant sentiment to a distinct national ideal in Québec, the rhetorical opportunities for opposition to immigration are also more limited.

Still, the differences in discourse are real, and we may ask why they do not in themselves have more significant effects. To explain this issue, I suggest we consider two factors. The first concerns the difference between symbolic and social group boundaries.

Discourse is essentially symbolic but in actual inter-group interactions in the community other factors often matter more. Basic values of fairness and equity are similar across the three settings.

The second factor is something we often forget: most members of minority groups, like people in general, are fairly apolitical. They tend to their daily affairs and form relations within more accepting segments of mainstream society. They make friends and work without confronting extreme views in their everyday lives. They are aware of public discourse, they discuss it in pubs and cafes, but then they go about their business.

The significance of religion in our thinking about immigration is to a large extent a matter of social construction. Muslim religion does not seem to pose nearly the barrier to integration as compared to (say) visible minority status. Kazemipur (2014: 180) argues correctly that regarding the "Muslim question," the best policy is to "shift our attention from the theological to the social." The prevailing focus on religion diverts attention from areas of life most critical to immigrant integration: getting a job, sending children to school, playing a role in community decision-making, and so on. The priority should be removing these barriers to integration, not legitimating new ones.

I think these conclusions matter for projecting the future of Canadian immigration. The lesson of comparative research is that while multicultural values mean something, they do not guarantee success if the underlying economic aspects of Canadian immigration are forgotten. The economic benefit of immigration derives from selection of immigrants on the basis of employability and the provision of assistance to help immigrants overcome employment and other barriers to integration. The current government projects substantially increased immigration over the next few years. The prospect of gradually increasing numbers from about 250,000, maintained consistently over the past 25 years, to 350,000 or even 450,000, has been discussed as a realistic possibility. Canada has successfully managed increases of this magnitude before with no loss in public support for immigration. In such periods, Canada maintained a sharp focus on the employment success of immigrants. The main lesson of comparative research is that this focus is bound to be of paramount importance in the future.

References

Alba, R. and N. Foner. 2015. *Strangers No More: Immigration and the Challenges of Integration in North America and Western Europe*. Princeton: Princeton University Press.
Allonier, C., P. Dourgnon, and T. Rochereau. 2010. "Enquête sur la santé et la protection sociale 2008." Paris : Institut de recherche et documentation en économie de la santé (IRDES).
Attewell, P., P. Kasinitz, and K. Dunn. 2010. "Black Canadians and Black Americans: Racial Income Inequality in Comparative Perspective," *Ethnic and Racial Studies* 33(3): 473-495.
Banting, K. and S. Soroka. 2012. "Minority Nationalism and Immigrant Integration in Canada." *Nations and Nationalism* 18(1): 156-176.
Beauchemin, C., C. Hamel, and P. Simon. 2015. *Trajectoires et origines: Enquête sur la diversité des populations en France*. Paris: INED. (Preliminary English publication: *Trajectories and Origins: Survey on Population Diversity in France, Initial Findings*. Paris: INED Documents de travail 168.
Béland, Y. 2002. Canadian Community Health Survey—Methodological Overview." *Health Reports* 13(3). Statistics Canada, Catalogue 82-003.
Bowen, J. 2007. "A View from France on the Internal Complexity of National Models." *Journal of Ethnic and Migration Studies* 33(6): 1003-1016.
The Economist. 2016. "Liberty moves north: it is uniquely fortunate in many ways—but Canada still holds lessons for other Western countries." 29 October.
German Marshall Fund of the United States. 2011. *Transatlantic Trends: Immigration—Key Findings 2010*. Washington, DC: German Marshall Fund of the United States.
Ishaq, Z. 2015. "Why I intend to wear a niqab at my citizenship ceremony," *Toronto Star*. 16 March. https://www.thestar.com/opinion/commentary/2015/03/16/why-i-intend-to-wear-a-niqab-at-my-citizenship-ceremony.html.
Joly, M.-P. and J. G. Reitz. 2016. "Emotional Stress and the Integration of Muslim Minorities in France, Québec and Anglophone Canada." Paper presented at an International Workshop "Muslim Integration in Europe and North America: New Directions in Comparative Research," 26-27 November. Paris: Fondation maison des sciences de l'homme (FMSH).
Kassir, A. and J. G. Reitz. 2016. "Protesting headscarf ban: a path to becoming more French? A case study of 'Mamans toutes égales' and 'Sorties scolaires avec nous.' *Ethnic and Racial Studies* 39(15): 2683-2700.
Kazemipur, A. 2014. *The Muslim Question in Canada: A Story of Segmented Integration*. Vancouver: UBC Press.
Kymlicka, W. 2012. *Multiculturalism: Success, Failure, and the Future*. Washington, DC: Migration Policy Institute.
Laxer, E. and J. Reitz. 2016. "Do National Integration Discourses Affect Muslims' Political and Civic Incorporation? A Comparison of France, Québec and the Rest of Canada." Paper presented at an International Workshop "Muslim Integration in Europe and North America: New Directions in Comparative Research," 26-27 November. Paris: Fondation maison des sciences de l'homme (FMSH), Paris.
Migrant Integration Policy Index. 2015. http://www.mipex.eu/.
Reitz, J.G. 2014. "Multiculturalism Policies and Popular Multiculturalism in the Development of Canadian Immigration." Pp. 107-126 in *The Multiculturalism Question: Debating Identity in 21st Century Canada*, Jack Jedwab, ed. Kingston: School of Policy Studies, Queen's University.
Reitz, J., M. Phan, and R. Banerjee. 2015. "Gender Equity in Canada's Newly Growing Religious Minorities," *Ethnic and Racial Studies*, 38(5): 681-699.
Reitz, J., P. Simon, and E. Laxer. Forthcoming. "Muslims' Social Inclusion and Exclusion in France, Québec and Canada: Does National Context Matter?" *Journal of Ethnic and Migration Studies*.
Statistics Canada. 2003. *Ethnic Diversity Survey: Portrait of a Multicultural Society*.

Catalogue no. 89-593-XIE.
United Nations. 2009. *International Migration Report 2006: A Global Assessment.* New York: United Nations Department of Economic and Social Affairs, Population Division. New York: United Nations. http://www.un.org/esa/population/publications/2006_MigrationRep/exec_sum.pdf.
van Reekum, J.W. Duyvendak, and C. Bertossi. 2012. "National models of integration and the crisis of multiculturalism: a critical comparative perspective." *Patterns of Prejudice* 46(5): 417-538.

CHAPTER FOUR
Race, Religion, and Citizenship Capital: Comment on Alba and Reitz

Naomi Lightman

In Canada, the United States, and Europe, anxieties about immigrant "integration," "acculturation" and "inclusion" are widespread and growing (Li 2003, Newman 2013 Sainsbury 2012). They are accompanied by heated debates about "reasonable accommodation" (Bouchard and Taylor 2008), struggles over—and sometimes backlash against—"multiculturalism" (Vertovec and Wessendorf 2010), and assertions of "ethnic" nationalism (Bloemraad, Korteweg, and Yurdakul 2008). The failure or refusal to assimilate to a dominant norm has been used to justify discrimination and marginalization (Good Gingrich 2016). An October 2016 CBC-Angus Reid Institute poll found that Canadians want minorities to do more to "fit in" and are more supportive of immigrant assimilation than are their American counterparts (Proctor 2016).

Despite these troubling realities, Alba and Reitz each present a largely positive picture of minority group inclusion. They suggest that through an expansion of the mainstream, many groups will ultimately be incorporated into the majority society. They further suggest that this will typically occur while minorities simultaneously maintain their prior ethnic distinction to some degree. This conclusion accords with a "neo-assimilationist" paradigm (Alba and Nee 1997).

Each author identifies one salient and persistent axis of exclusion. Alba finds that *race*, and specifically being Black in the United States, is a marker of ongoing exclusion. His data indicate that mixed-race individuals with a Black parent, particularly a Black father, show different patterns of intermarriage and economic mobility than do Hispanic or Asian mixed-race people. Other researchers find similar patterns of "segmented" assimilation (Portes 1995) for African-origin Blacks in Canada and numerous Black groups in France and elsewhere in Europe (Creese and Wiebe 2012, Silverman 2002).

For his part, Reitz focuses on *religion* as a salient axis of exclusion, examining integration outcomes for Muslim populations in France, Québec and the rest of Canada. He notes that these groups have been targeted and rejected by some members of majority populations through physical violence and acts of policy.

Alba and Reitz thus argue that race and religion remain important markers of inclusion in, and exclusion from, majority White and Judeo-Christian societies. Yet they also suggest that there is room for optimism if we consider trends over time, specifically with regard to the second and third generations.

I propose that, in addition to race and religion, a third salient axis of exclusion for immigrants and their offspring appears to be growing in importance. It is tied to immigrants' form of entry. I refer to this axis of exclusion as migrants' *citizenship capital* (Lightman and Bejan 2014). By citizenship capital, I mean the myriad ways that migration trajectories and legal statuses may lead to the dispossession and devaluation of financial, social and cultural capital.

In assessing the importance of citizenship capital, I consider three questions: Are the migrants in question legal or illegalized?[1] Are they permanent or non-permanent residents, and are they provided a pathway to citizenship? Do they enter the country as refugees fleeing persecution or as economic immigrants with attendant human capital? Certainly, the resulting citizenship capital accumulated by each immigrant intersects significantly with their race, religion and economic class. However, I suggest that including analysis of the form of entry in studies of immigrant integration may lead to evidence of growing social divides, diminishing to some degree existing findings of immigrant and minority group integration.

The Different Forms of Citizenship Capital

Bourdieu (1990) defines three types of capital that are circulated and reproduced in everyday social relations and practices: economic, social and cultural. Citizenship capital, which can be conceptu-

---

[1]. I follow Bauder (2014), who uses "illegalized" rather than "illegal" or "undocumented" to emphasize how state policies render migrants illegal, suggesting that only actions, not individuals, can be illegal.

alized as a component of cultural capital, takes on different forms in different contexts but influences opportunities for upward mobility and broader social inclusion (Good Gingrich and Lightman 2015). Alba and Foner (2017) note that the phrase "new Americans" nearly always refers to those legally resident in the country. Certainly, immigration status determines rights and entitlements, some of which are transmitted between generations and influence opportunities for upward mobility. For example, migrants without status are illegalized, paying into a country's tax base when they buy goods and services but typically unable to receive most welfare state benefits.

Examples of how citizenship capital affects public discourse and minority group integration are myriad. In the United States, President Trump has spoken repeatedly about the need to "build a wall" to keep out "illegal Mexicans." During his election campaign he repeatedly mentioned that "illegal" immigrants (mostly Hispanic in the American context) perform criminal acts and are stealing jobs from "legitimate" immigrants. In the European Union, most recent laws pertaining to immigration seek to prevent migrants lacking the necessary documentation from entering the EU and facilitating their expulsion if they do. Often, such actions take place at the expense of migrants' human rights (Cholewinski 2006).

Canadians are less concerned about illegalized migration because we lack a border with a Global South country. However, much of the discourse on citizenship capital in Canada is focused on residency status. In Canada there is increasing reliance on temporary foreign workers, both skilled and those deemed unskilled, as well as a resultant backlash again temporary migrants for allegedly taking jobs away from Canadian citizens.[2] While in Canada, temporary foreign workers are not entitled to federally funded settlement services or most other government-related assistance, including language training, public health care, Employment Insurance, and Canada Pension Plan benefits (Fang and MacPhail 2008; Fudge and MacPhail 2009). Because temporary foreign workers lack the

---

2. A widely-circulated C.D. Howe Institute report stated that the Temporary Foreign Worker (TFW) program had spurred joblessness among Canadians in British Columbia and Alberta (Gross 2014). Media attention resulted in an immediate month-long moratorium on the fast-food industry's access to the TFW program. Calls grew for "Canadians first" in employment (Goodman 2014) and temporary foreign workers as a "last and limited" resort (Curry 2014).

rights and entitlements that are attached to permanent residency, Goldring and Landolt (2011: 327) note that "complex institutional and geographic pathways leave migrants vulnerable for increasingly long periods of time during which they must navigate 'insecure migratory legal status.'"

In addition to illegalized and temporary statuses, another dimension of citizenship capital is evident in the sharpening divide between refugees and "traditional" economic immigrants worldwide. In the Canadian context, former Prime Minister Stephen Harper often remarked on the supposed threat of "bogus refugees" and "queue jumpers" who were allegedly manipulating the Canadian immigration system to their benefit and abusing the social service system. In France, the Calais refugee camp was colloquially known as the "jungle" camp, where migrants lived in horrible conditions while seeking to claim refugee status in the UK, where economic prospects were more favourable than on the Continent. And in the United States, Donald Trump and his supporters have proclaimed the need to ban Syrian refugees from entering the country altogether. Thus, in the case of Syrian refugees, religion, race and immigrant form of entry intersect to prevent refugees from integrating into their chosen places of relocation.

Citizenship Capital and the Problem of Measurement

I have no doubt that both Alba and Reitz would be eager to measure the effects of citizenship capital in each of their respective analyses were it possible. Unfortunately, major challenges prohibit our ability to adequately measure citizenship capital. This predicament obscures the effect of what is likely an important marker of minority exclusion.

In qualitative studies, it is often difficult to disentangle the influence of overlapping factors. Is exclusion due to racism? Islamophobia? Precarious legal status or a fear of deportation? Anecdotal evidence may provide inconsistent findings.

In large-scale quantitative analyses, such as those conducted by Alba and Reitz, variables needed to measure the influence of citizenship capital are often unavailable because representative samples of the population typically include few or no illegalized migrants. Moreover, illegalized migrants are reluctant to disclose information for fear of deportation and other penalties.

Thus, the data that we have measuring the effects of migrant form of entry is frequently inaccurate or partial. This situation allows public opinion about such migrants to be shaped by preconceptions rather than appropriately interpreted facts, invigorating xenophobia and fear of low potential for minority integration.

One consequence of the lack of relevant data is that the most dispossessed migrants often remain uncounted and therefore invisible. And the more extreme the global divide between the "haves" and the "have-nots" in terms of citizenship capital as well as other ascriptive characteristics, the less our ability to describe the realities of migrants' lives and the social processes that contribute to them: "That which is not seen cannot be represented or measured, in qualitative or quantitative terms" (Good Gingrich and Lightman 2015: 107).

In sum, Bourdieu's ideas allow us to begin developing the concept of citizenship capital and emphasize the growing importance of immigrants' form of entry in analyses of minority integration. I have stressed the significance of citizenship capital in conjunction with axes of exclusion based on race and religion, specifically in the case of Blacks and Muslims. I suggest that current studies of immigrant integration likely overestimate the extent of minority group incorporation by excluding from consideration variables that measure citizenship capital.

References

Alba, Richard and Victor Nee. 1997. "Rethinking Assimilation Theory for a New Era of Immigration." *International Migration Review* 31(4): 826-74.

Alba, Richard and Nancy Foner. 2017. *Strangers No More: Immigration and the Challenges of Integration in North America and Western Europe*. Princeton, New Jersey: Princeton University Press.

Bauder, Harald. 2014. "Why We Should Use the Term 'Illegalized' Refugee or Immigrant: A Commentary." *International Journal of Refugee Law* 26(3): 327-32.

Bloemraad, Irene, Anna Korteweg and Gökçe Yurdakul. 2008. "Citizenship and Immigration: Multiculturalism, Assimilation, and Challenges to the Nation-State." *Annual Review of Sociology* 34(1): 153-79.

Bouchard, Gérard and Charles Taylor. 2008. "Building the Future. A Time for Reconciliation. Report of the Consultation Commission on Accommodation Practices Related to Cultural Differences." Quebec: Government of Quebec.

Bourdieu, Pierre. 1990. *The Logic of Practice*. Palo Alto, CA: Stanford University Press.

Cholewinski, Ryszard. 2006. "Control of Irregular Migration and EU Law and Policy: A Human Rights Deficit." Pp. 899-942 in *EU Immigration and Asylum Law*. Leiden and Boston: Brill Publishers.

Creese, Gillian and Brandy Wiebe. 2012. "'Survival Employment': Gender and Deskilling among African Immigrants in Canada." *International Migration* 50(5): 56-76.

Curry, Bill. 2014. "Temporary Foreign Worker Ban Will Hurt Tourist Trade, Restaurateurs Warn." *Globe and Mail*, 27 May.

Fang, Tony and Fiona MacPhail. 2008. "Transitions from Temporary to Permanent Work in Canada: Who Makes the Transition and Why?" *Social Indicators Research* 88: 51-74.

Fudge, Judy and Fiona MacPhail. 2009. "The Temporary Foreign Worker Program in Canada: Low-Skilled Workers as an Extreme Form of Flexible Labour." *Comparative Labor Law and Policy Journal* 31(1): 101-39.

Good Gingrich, Luann and Naomi Lightman. 2015. "The Empirical Measurement of a Theoretical Concept: Tracing Social Exclusion among Racial Minority and Migrant Groups in Canada." *Social Inclusion* 3(4): 98-111.

Good Gingrich, Luann. 2016. *Out of Place: Social Exclusion and Mennonite Migrants in Canada*. Toronto: University of Toronto Press.

Goodman, Lee-Anne. 2014. "Kenney Imposes Partial Moratorium on Temporary Foreign Workers Program." Global News, 24 April.

Gross, Dominique M. 2014. "Temporary Foreign Workers in Canada: Are They Really Filling Labour Shortages?" C.D. Howe Institute, Commentary No. 407.

Li, Peter S. 2003. "Deconstructing Canada's Discourse of Immigrant Integration." *Journal of International Migration and Integration* 4(3): 315-33.

Lightman, Naomi and Raluca Bejan. 2014. "Factually Mapping Harper's Policy of Revised Immigration Control." Conference presentation at *Southern Political Science Association, 85th Annual Meeting*. New Orleans.

Newman, Benjamin J. 2013. "Acculturating Contexts and Anglo Opposition to Immigration in the United States." *American Journal of Political Science* 57(2): 374-90.

Portes, Alejandro. 1995. "Children of Immigrants: Segmented Assimilation and Its Determinants." Pp. 248-79 in *The Economic Sociology of Immigration: Essays on Networks, Ethnicity and Entrepreneurship*, edited by A. Portes. New York: Russell Sage Foundation.

Sainsbury, Diane. 2012. *Welfare States and Immigrant Rights: The Politics of Inclusion and Exclusion*. New York: Oxford University Press.

Silverman, Maxim. 2002. *Deconstructing the Nation: Immigration, Racism and Citizenship in Modern France. London: Routledge.

Vertovec, Steven and Susanne Wessendorf. 2010. *The Multiculturalism Backlash: European Discourses, Policies and Practices.* London: Routledge.

Part Two
ISSUES IN CANADIAN IMMIGRATION

CHAPTER FIVE
Second Generation Educational and Occupational Attainment in Canada

Monica Boyd

Framing the Topic

Throughout the 20th century and early 21st centuries, the number of migrants coming to Canada fluctuated dramatically (Boyd and Vickers 2016, Figure 12.1). Today, one in five Canadians is foreign born and growth in the proportion of foreign-born Canadians shows no sign of abating. Projections estimate that by 2036 at least one in four Canadians will be foreign born (Morency, Malenfant, and MacIsaac 2017). Such demographic trends substantiate the importance of immigration for Canada's nation building, both historically and today. Immigrants represent a vital source of population growth—of workers, innovators, and consumers (Boyd and Alboim 2012).

In addition to their own contributions to Canada, immigrants are the parents of future generations. The second generation—those who are Canadian born but have at least one foreign-born parent—is sizeable: 18 percent of Canadians in 2011. Shifts in the country origins of parents also mean that growing shares are visible minorities: 30 percent of the second generation in 2011 and expected to reach 50 percent or more by 2036 (Morency, Malenfant, and MacIsaac, 2017). These demographic statistics reflect national trends. The proportion of the population that is second generation and the share that is non-White are higher in large cities where the immigrant parental generation originally settled.

Those belonging to the second generation are of particular sociological interest because their experience speaks to two related themes of immigration and stratification research: improving life chances and who gets what and why (Jasso 2011). Migrants usually cross international borders to improve their situation, raising the question of what their lives are really like after migrating. In answering this question, many stratification scholars focus on socio-economic integration, studying the relationships between education, occupations, and earnings, which, in turn, are correlated with indicators of well-being, such as health, poverty, wealth accumulation, and quality of housing and neighbourhoods. Extensive research on the socio-economic integration of migrants in Canada indicates that recently arrived immigrants experience labour market difficulties, especially compared to the Canadian-born population. In particular, data analyses of large surveys (usually the census) find educational credentials and work experience outside Canada are devalued for recent immigrants, and their earnings are lower than those of comparable Canadian-born groups (Frenette and Morissette 2005; Hou and Picot 2016; Picot and Sweetman 2005). Audit studies, which send contrived résumés to would-be employers, also suggest that immigrants face hiring barriers based on their origin, race, and language proficiency (Dechief and Oreopoulos 2012).

Consequently, immigration scholars now say it is not enough to study only the integration of immigrants. Instead, they urge reaching across generations to study the socio-economic integration of the children of migrants. A major objective is to determine if the children also experience difficulties in educational attainment and in the labour market.

There are reasons to think the educational attainment and labour market experience of the second generation should be much like that of people further removed from the migration experience, notably the third-plus generation, that is, people who are Canadian-born with Canadian-born parents (with many having Canadian-born grandparents and great-grandparents). Both the second and third-plus generations are exposed as youngsters to the destination country's school system, language(s), media, culture, and labour market institutions. According to stratification experts, in a meritocratic society, the difficulties experienced by migrant parents should not extend across generations, and people should be employed and paid according to their education, training, skill, and occupation. That said, there is concern, supported by audit studies and surveys asking respondents to report their experiences and perceptions of discrimination, that non-Whites in the second gen-

eration encounter discrimination and barriers in the workplace.
Research on the second generation is extensive, including studies of children in school and studies that assess multiple dimensions of integration, including identity, feelings of belonging, and transnational ties. In this chapter, I consider only the socioeconomic situation of the second generation, focusing on the educational and occupational attainment of young adults. I address three important issues. First, I ask how well the second generation does relative to the third-plus generation on these two socio-economic dimensions. Reflecting the changing origins of recent immigrants to Canada and employment equity legislation introduced in 1986, I also ask if the conclusions reached by comparing the entire second and third-plus generations hold when distinctions are made by race. Second, I address the theme of "who gets what and why" by asking what factors likely produce the findings. To do so, I summarize recent studies that analyze large Canadian surveys and present my own findings from the 2011 National Household Survey. (Data from the 2016 census have not yet been released by Statistics Canada.) I end by briefly indicating where new avenues of future research exist.

Educational Attainment and the Second Generation
Education is a pathway to increased knowledge, skill development, and ultimately to jobs. If elementary and secondary schooling provide essential skills in the form of literacy, numeracy, and basic knowledge of science, social science, and the humanities, then post-secondary education—particularly university education—is even more desirable, since it provides specialized training and new knowledge (Hirschman 2016). Higher education can lead to lower rates of unemployment, better jobs, higher status occupations, and higher earnings.

Today's immigrants often have university degrees because admission criteria emphasize their potential economic contribution and use higher education as an admissibility criterion (Boyd 2014; Boyd and Alboim 2012). But what about their children who are born in Canada? One of the most consistent findings in recent Canadian social science research is the educational over-achievement of the second generation compared to the third-plus generations in adulthood. Obtaining at least a university degree is usually the indicator used in this research; far less attention is paid to other forms of post-secondary education (Abada, Hou, and Ram 2009; Abada and Tenkorang 2009; Boyd 2002; 2009; Aydemir and Sweetman 2008; Picot and Hou 2010).[1] Several studies examine very young adults, finding that the children of immigrants have higher aspirations for university and are more likely to attend university than their non-immigrant counterparts (Childs, Finnie, and Mueller 2015; Taylor and Krahn 2005).

The higher educational attainment of the second generation compared to the third-plus generation is evident in recent data from Statistics Canada, namely the 2011 National Household Survey, which surveyed about one in three households. Figure 5.1 shows the percentages with bachelor's degrees for the second and third-plus generations aged 25-64. People in this age range have for the most part completed schooling and represent the core working-age population. In this age cohort, 21 percent of the third-plus generation has a university degree or higher compared to 31 percent of the second generation. The chart also shows that younger age cohorts tend to have higher levels of education. But across all age cohorts, the second generation has higher percentages obtaining at least bachelor's degrees.

What factors underlie these patterns? To ask the question differently, why does higher educational achievement exist for the second generation but not the third-plus generation? One factor influencing how far people go in school is geography. Generally speaking, people who grow up in large communities are more likely to have higher education, if only because larger communities house universities and other institutions of higher learning. This observation is useful when comparing the educational attainment of the second and third-plus generations; as the children of immigrants, those in the second generation are far more likely to have grown up in one of Canada's three largest cities (Toronto, Montre-

---

[1]. Probable reasons for the focus on a university degree include its importance in a knowledge economy; a "sheepskin effect" in which analysts and survey respondents alike prize the awarding of a degree; and the need to use a common measure when undertaking comparative research between Canada and the United States (Adyemir and Sweetman 2008; Picot and Hou 2010; for an exception, see Reitz, Zhang, and Hawkins 2011). Changes by Statistics Canada to the 2006 census education question removed the ability to calculate years of schooling, thus accentuating future reliance on obtaining a university bachelor's degree as a measure of higher education.

al, and Vancouver) than those in the third-plus generation. When this fact is taken into account, the size of the gap decreases, although the second generation is still more likely to hold university degrees than is the third-plus generation (Boyd 2002; 2009; Picot and Hou 2010).

Another body of explanations emphasizes the impact of immigrant parents. Three inter-related variants exist: Canada got lucky; the migrants selected for admission are better educated than those left in the origin country and better educated than many Canadian residents; and the aspirations of immigrant parents influence their children's educational attainment.

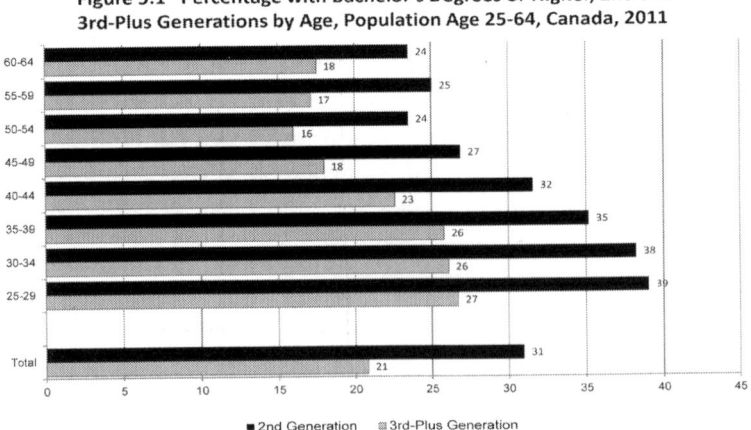

Figure 5.1 Percentage with Bachelor's Degrees or Higher, 2nd and 3rd-Plus Generations by Age, Population Age 25-64, Canada, 2011

Age	2nd Generation	3rd-Plus Generation
60-64	18	24
55-59	17	25
50-54	16	24
45-49	18	27
40-44	23	32
35-39	26	35
30-34	26	38
25-29	27	39
Total	21	31

Source: Computed from Statistics Canada, 2011 National Household Survey Public Use File, Individuals.

The "Canada got lucky" perspective alludes to changing immigration policy regimes since the 1970s. The trend toward ever-higher levels of education among immigrants continues as Canada seeks to admit the best and the brightest (Boyd 2014; Boyd and Alboim 2012). Students of stratification note that well educated parents tend to have well educated children simply because the parents are familiar with higher education systems, expect their children at least to reproduce parental levels of attainment, and tend to have the resources needed to interface with schools and teachers and to assist with school-related tasks such as homework. In short, better educated parents tend to have better educated children, and Canada "got lucky" when it admitted many highly-educated immigrant parents.

The second variant of this perspective emphasizes that policy was more important than luck in ensuring this outcome. Canadian immigrants are not randomly chosen. They are unusual relative to the populations in which they originated in terms of their education, talent, IQ, or other unmeasured qualities. Canadian immigration policy is designed to ensure that a disproportionately large number of such exceptional people are admitted to the country and often they are better educated than their fellow Canadians.

The third variant of this perspective holds that immigrant parents' relatively high level of education likely influences the educational outcomes of their children. It does so in two ways. First, immigrant parents may possess cultural capital such as foreign language skills and appreciation for classical music that may influence their children's educational outcomes. They also have a subjectively higher social status based on their position in the origin countries, and this is related to higher educational expectations (Feliciano 2005; 2006; Feliciano and Lanuza 2016; Ichou 2014). Highly educated immigrants may thus import from their home countries cultural institutions and practices designed to maximize the educational success of their children. Lee and Zhou (2015) find that Chinese parents in the United States tend to rely on after-school academies and courses that prepare students for SAT tests to enhance the educational potential of their sons and daughters. How generalizable this explanation is for other groups and across borders requires investigation. Bonikowska's (2007) Canadian research on the educational attainment of the second generation argues that cultural explanations are not convincing; she refers to the argument that parents may come from countries where education is highly valued and that this cultural emphasis explains the educational attainment of children.

All these explanations are newer and more nuanced extensions of the familiar view that family background influences the social position of children. Certainly, Canadian studies confirm that parental educational level influences the educational attainment of the second generation (Abada, Hou and Ram 2009; Aydemir and Sweetman 2008; Aydemir, Chen, and Corak 2013; Boyd 2002;

Chen and Hou 2016; Finnie and Mueller 2010; Picot and Hou 2010). However, these studies all find that parental education is only part of what explains the high percentage of the second generation holding at least a bachelor's degree. Even when allowances are made for differences between generations in parental education and demographic characteristics (such as place of residence as a child), members of the second generation are more likely to have university degrees than are members of the third-plus generation. Further, the children of less well educated parents drive the higher educational attainment of the second generation (Picot and Hou 2010). Said differently, there is normally an association between the education of the parents and that of the offspring—the children of highly educated parents tend to be highly educated, partly because of greater familial resources, while the children of less well-educated parents do not advance as far on the education trajectory. But studies confirm that this association is weaker for the second generation than for the third-plus generation, implying

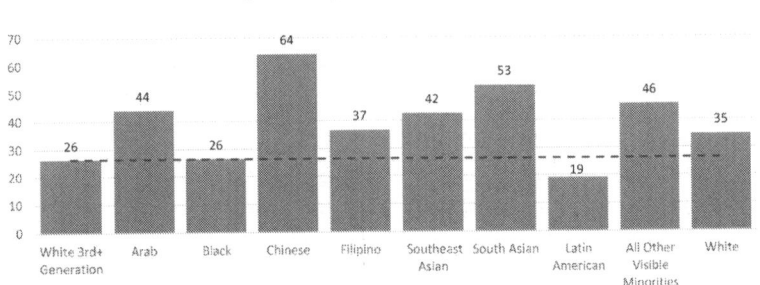

Figure 5.2 **Percentage with Bachelor's Degree or Higher by Generation and Visible Minority Status, Age 25-39, Canada, 2011**

Group	%
White 3rd+ Generation	26
Arab	44
Black	26
Chinese	64
Filipino	37
Southeast Asian	42
South Asian	53
Latin American	19
All Other Visible Minorities	46
White	35

Source: Computed from Statistics Canada, 2011 National Household Survey Public Use File, Individuals.

that second-generation children from less well-educated families graduate from university to a much greater extent than might be expected (Aydemir, Chen, and Corak 2013; Boyd 2002; Hoe 2012; Picot and Hou 2010).

How are we to understand the higher educational attainment of the second generation, measured here as the likelihood of getting at least a bachelor's degree? Census data and most large-scale surveys do not ask the questions necessary to tap into the contexts of the educational decisions made by the second generation and their parents.[2] However, several Canadian and U.S. studies indicate that the second generation attains a high level of education because of parental expectations and aspirations for their children, which, in turn, are acquired by the offspring. As noted by Childs, Finnie, and Mueller (2015: 3) in their analysis of Canadian data on university attendance: "Somehow the idea of going to university is so ingrained in these youth by their immigrant parents that they find the means to attend, even when, statistically speaking, they should not." Similarly, Picot and Hou (2013, Table 2) find that parental expectations and student hopes for university completion are the most important factors behind university attendance, far

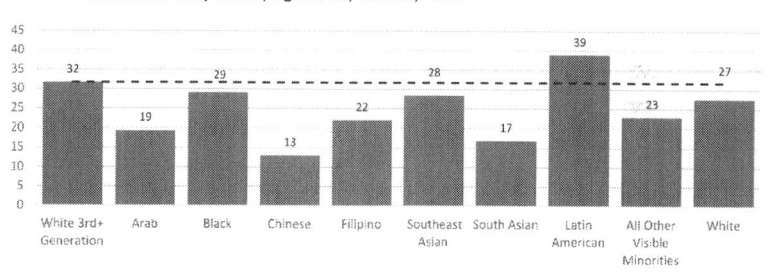

Figure 5.3 Percentage with No Postsecondary Degree, by Generation and Visible Minority Status, Age 25-39, Canada, 2011

Group	%
White 3rd+ Generation	32
Arab	19
Black	29
Chinese	13
Filipino	22
Southeast Asian	28
South Asian	17
Latin American	39
All Other Visible Minorities	23
White	27

Source: Computed from Statistics Canada, 2011 National Household Survey Public Use File, Individuals.

exceeding the impact of parental education. The result is that the second generation over-achieves educationally compared with the third-plus generation.[3]

The Educational Attainments of Second Generation Visible Minorities

So far I have focused on the attainment of bachelor's degrees by the second generation without considering the considerable diversity of the second generation. In fact, the increased migration of immi-

---

2. Some researchers also call attention to the importance of ethnic resources as a factor motivating the second generation to obtain bachelor's degrees. However, such studies rely on crude, aggregate indicators such as the percentage of a specific ethnic group residing in a city.

3. This comparative pattern is called the "success orientation model" (Boyd and Grieco 1998) or the "immigrant optimism hypothesis" (Kao and Tienda 1995). It contrasts with the more orthodox "linear assimilation" model in which the second generation does better than its parents but less well than the third-plus generation. The latter model is based on early 20th century migration in which migrants came from agricultural communities and had far less education than the population born in destination areas. It is less applicable in a time when countries seek to recruit the best and the brightest migrants for permanent residency.

grants from Asia, Latin America, the Caribbean, and Africa means that visible minorities are now a key part of the second generation. The term "visible minority" was first used in the early 1980s in Canada to denote groups that are distinctive by virtue of their race or colour. The term is socially constructed in that its origins lie in discussions of, and legislation on, employment equity and related program requirements in the 1980s. Visible minorities are defined in the census as people who self-identify as Chinese, South Asian (e.g., East Indian, Pakistani, Sri Lankan, etc.), Black, Filipino, Latin American, Southeast Asian (e.g., Vietnamese, Cambodian, Malaysian, Laotian, etc.), Arab, West Asian (e.g., Iranian, Afghan, etc.), Korean, Japanese, and Other (as specified by the respondent). However, these sub-groups combine people from socially diverse locales—for example, those self-identifying as Chinese may have origins in Malaysia, Taiwan, Hong Kong, China, or elsewhere. Colour labels such as Black or pan-geographic labels such as South Asian and Latin American also mask substantial within-group diversity.

The increasing focus in Canadian immigration research on racial stratification usually examines the educational and labour market outcomes for visible minorities in relation to those of the White majority population. When discussing the second generation, this comparison means contrasting select visible-minority, second-generation groups to the third-plus, White generation. In such comparisons it is important to recognize that the shift in the origin composition of immigrants only started in the 1970s, and most members of the visible-minority second generation are young (Boyd 2017, Table 1). In the working age population, aged 25-64, most second-generation visible minorities are in their late twenties and early thirties, whereas the White third-plus generation is most likely to be between the ages of 40 and 65. Consequently, comparisons of educational attainment for working age adults aged 25-64 risk distorting conclusions by comparing people who by virtue of their youth have higher levels of education to those who are older and who may have less education (see Figure 5.1). The caution also holds for indicators of labour market integration such as occupation and earnings. This age distortion holds for any race-specific assessment of how the second generation is doing in the labour force. As a result, most studies focus on those aged 25-39 or 25-44. The age restriction means that members of the second and third-plus generation were born between 1957 and 1976 if data are from surveys fielded in 2001—or between 1967 and 1986 if data are from the 2011 National Household Survey (using the age range 25-44). These dates indicate that analyses conducted so[3] far examine the experiences of a unique cohort, notably those whose parents arrived before 1985 and often much earlier.

Within the research on the Canadian second generation, educational attainment is the most frequently studied variable. Investigations into the educational attainment of young visible-minority adults consistently find that compared to the third-plus generation, the second generation exhibits a pattern in which Chinese and South Asians tend to have above-average levels of university attainment and Blacks and Latin Americans have below-average levels of university attainment (Abada, Hou, and Ram 2009; Abada and Tenkorang 2009; Boyd 2017; Boyd and Tian 2016; Chen and Hou 2016; Kelly 2014; Reitz, Zhang, and Hawkins 2011). These conclusions rest mainly on analyses of data from around 2001-02. Figure 5.2 updates this pattern using data from the 2011 National Household Survey for the 25-39 age cohort. It shows that in 2011 the percentage of Black, second-generation Canadians with a bachelor's degree was equal to that of the White third-plus generation. However, the corresponding percentage for Latin Americans was lower than that of the White third-plus generation.[4] All other second-generation groups had higher corresponding percentages than that of the White third-plus generation. Figure 5.3 highlights the other end of the educational distribution by showing the percentage of people who failed to attain a high school degree. Latin American visible-minority second generation young adults had the highest percentage without a high school degree.[5]

---

4. In their analysis of data from the 2002 Ethnic Diversity Survey and eight General Social Surveys fielded between 2003 and 2014, Chen and Hou (2016) find all visible minority groups, including Blacks and Latin Americans, have higher percentages attaining bachelor's degrees than the White third-plus generation. However, they focus on the 25-44 age cohort rather than the 25-39 age cohort. The additional five years may affect their findings because the White third-plus generation is older in their analysis and is likely to have less education because of the relationship between education and age cohort.

5. Results not presented here show that Latin American and Black second-generation men are less likely than White third-plus generation men to acquire bachelor's degrees.

Most analyses of large data sets that highlight visible-minority group variations shed little light on why second-generation visible minorities do or do not acquire bachelor's degrees. The most extensive investigations generally use the 2002 Ethnic Diversity Survey to see if educational variation among ethnic and racial groups reflects parental education, growing up in a single-parent family, language while growing up, place of parental residence, and ethnic capital (crudely defined as an ethnic group's average level of education and the ethnic group's average family income; see Abada, Hou and Ram 2009; Abada and Tenkorang 2009; Picot and Hou 2010).[6] Level of parental education is an important factor in raising the education of the various ethnic and racial groups. However, it matters less for those of the second generation from Western societies. Most likely, the reasons found to influence education levels—parental education, expectations and aspirations—still hold. One study of Toronto District School Board data observes that higher family socio-economic status (defined by parental education and occupation) is important for high school youth transitioning to university (Sweet et. al. 2009), noting that lower family socio-economic status depresses the university pathway of young, Black high school students. At the same time, a second study argues that the aspirations of 15-year-old visible minority youth are much higher than those of their native-born, non-visible minority counterparts (Taylor and Krahn 2005).

Making a Living: The Link between Education and Occupation

As discussed earlier, one reason researchers focus on formal education is that it indicates relative level of knowledge. Another is that it shows the extent to which individuals participate in one of Canada's major institutions. A third reason is that education is a form of human capital, representing the knowledge, skills, and training acquired by individuals through the educational system. According to economists, higher education usually means higher productivity and wages. As such, in post-industrial societies, educational attain-

---

6. Strictly speaking, the findings by Abada, Hou, and Ram (2009) from the 2002 Ethnic Diversity Survey are not limited to second generation visible minorities. The authors combine the 1.5 generation, consisting of those who are foreign-born but arrived as children, with the second generation. The focal groups are based on the survey questions on ethnic origins and race, and comparisons are between ethnic-racial groups and the second generation declaring British ethnic origin.

ment is associated with labour force participation, employment and unemployment, the types of occupations that people have, and their earnings. The role of education in the economic sector is so strong that, in the late 1960s, the status attainment paradigm saw it as mediating most if not all of the impact of family origin. In this view, family characteristics might matter for the life-chances of individuals but they do so by influencing level of educational attainment (Boyd et al. 1985).[7]

What are the occupational characteristics of the second generation compared to the third-plus generation, and how important is education in determining the occupational characteristics of the second generation? These questions can be answered with data from the 2011 National Household Survey. In this data base, the 500 occupational titles originally collected are collapsed into 30 occupational groupings. I use the 30 categories to define two types of occupational characteristics: employment in a high-skill occupation and occupational status.

The first indicator, employment in a high-skill occupation, is defined as employment in occupations that require university education (Statistics Canada, n.d.),[8] a definition first established by experts convened by Employment and Social Development Canada (then Human Development Canada) in the late 1980s. Unfortunately, for occupations in art, culture, recreation, and sport, the 2011 National Household Survey Microdata File on Individuals combines one set of occupations requiring university education with another set requiring only college education or apprenticeship training. Investigation shows most of the more detailed occupational titles found in the file's broad classification of "professional occupations and technical occupations in art, culture, recreation and sport" do not require a university education. As a result, this broad category is omitted from the list of occupations considered

---

7. This generalization still holds. Additionally, two studies examine the impact of parental characteristics on the earnings of Canadian immigrant offspring. However, the parental measures are pseudo-measures, obtained by generating distributions of likely parental characteristics from earlier census data and appending these to individual records. The analyses find a significant but small effect of fathers' earnings on the earnings of the 1.5 and second generation (Aydemir, Chen, and Corak 2009; Aydemir and Sweetman, 2008).

8. A few studies add those employed in management occupations to those defined as high-skill or professional occupations. Results are similar in that the second generation is more likely to be employed in the combined occupational classes (Reitz, Zhang, and Hawkins 2011).

to be high skill in my analysis.

I also employ a ranking of the 30 occupational groupings available in the 2011 National Household Survey Microdata File on Individuals (cf. Boyd 1998; 2008a; 2009). The score for each occupation indicates the location of that occupation in a hierarchical distribution that ranges from 0 to 100. Each score indicates the percentage of the entire labour force that is in occupations ranked below the given occupation. For example, a score of 53 associated with the category "Paraprofessional occupations in legal, social, community and education services" indicates that 53 percent of the entire labour force work in other occupations where the combined levels of education and earnings are lower than found for "Paraprofessional occupations in legal, social, community and education services." Higher scores are found for occupational groups where the combined education and earnings are high, and lower scores are found for occupational groups where educational levels and earnings are low.

My analysis confirms earlier findings. The entire second generation is more likely than the entire third-plus generation to work in high-skill occupations and, on average, members of this generation find themselves in occupations ranked higher in terms of composite educational and earnings characteristics. Twenty-five percent of the second generation in Canada works in an occupation that usually requires a university education compared to 20 percent of the third-plus generation. Likewise, the average occupational score for the second generation in Canada is 59.0 points, compared to 55.7 points for the third-plus generation. Analysis not presented here shows that the higher education of the second generation compared to the third-plus generation is most important in explaining the advantageous occupational score for the second generation, followed by differences between the two groups in location of residence (a proxy for local labour market characteristics), age, and other demographic variables.

Like those investigating the educational attainment of the children of immigrants, scholars considering the labour market integration of the second and third-plus generations ask if the occupational advantage holds for specific visible minorities. In fact, the overall patterns generally correspond to what might be expected on the basis of the educational characteristics of each visible minority group (Boyd 2008b; Boyd 2017; Boyd, Jeong, and Tian 2014; Chen and Hou 2016; Reitz, Zhang, and Hawkins 2011). My research confirms that education explains a great deal of the pattern observed for each group. Table 5.1 compares percentages with high-skilled occupations for visible minority groups in the second generation and the White third-plus generation.

Table 5.1. Regression of Holding High-Skill Occupation on Demographic and Educational Predictors,[a] Canada, 2011

		Deviations from the White 3rd-plus Generation		
		Model 1	Model 2	Model 3
Group	Actual Value	Actual Value	Demographic Characteristics[b]	Demographic & Educational Characteristics[c]
White, 3rd+ generation (rg)	19			
Arab, 2nd generation	28	9.0**	5.4	-4.1
Black, 2nd generation	18	-1.5	-4.0***	-4.3
Chinese, 2nd generation	40	21.0***	18.1***	-0.1**
Filipino, 2nd generation	26	7.4***	4.1*	-2.6
Other Southeast Asian, 2nd generation	28	8.8***	6.5*	-3.9
South Asian, 2nd generation	34	14.5***	11.4***	-1.2
Latin American, 2nd generation	14	-5.2	-7.2**	-5.2
Other visible minority, 2nd generation	24	4.6*	1.0	-6.0**
White, 2nd generation	22	3.3***	1.5***	-3.5**

*p<0.05; **p<0.01; ***p<0.001
rg = reference group
(a) For people age 25-39, not in school and with an occupation code.
(b) Demographic characteristics include sex, age, city of residence, province of residence, and marital status.
(c) Educational characteristics include highest educational level attained and field of study.

Note: Significance levels are for the logits produced from logistic regression using the indicator method.

Source: Computed from Statistics Canada, 2011 National Household Survey Public Use Microdata File on Individuals.

The basis of Table 5.1 is a logistic regression analysis. The first column ("Actual Value") shows all percentages in high-skill occupations, using Statistics Canada's National Occupational Classification of occupations requiring university education. The second column ("Model 1") presents the same data but in comparison with the White third-plus generation. For example, 19 percent of the White third-plus population who indicate their occupations say they are in high-skill occupations. The figure is 28 percent for the second generation who define themselves as Arab. As shown in column two, the difference is 9 percentage points. This "deviation" lets us see the differences more clearly. The deviations in the second column show that a high percentage of the Chinese and South Asian second generation have high-skill occupations compared to the White, third-plus generation. Model 2 shows what the differences would be if all groups had the same demographic characteristics with respect to sex composition, age, city of residence, province of residence, and marital status. If differences in these characteristics are taken into account, the deviations or differences between the visible-minority second generation and the third-plus White generation decrease slightly but do not disappear. Members of the Black and Latin American second-generation continue to have lower percentages in high-skill occupations relative to the third-plus White generation. All other second-generation visible-minority groups continue to have higher percentages in high-skill occupations relative to the White third-plus generation. This finding tells us that group differences in demographic characteristics matter somewhat but not enough to change the initial conclusion based on the actual deviations.

Model 3 shows what the differences would be if the groups had the same distribution of demographic characteristics *and* educational attainment and post-secondary field of study. If the overall higher educational attainments of the second generation did not exist, most of the differences in holding high-skill occupations would become minor. In fact, most of the deviations are within the range of random fluctuation; they are not statistically significant. In short, the higher educational levels and the fields of study distributions for the second generation are important factors explaining the greater tendency of the various second-generation minority groups to be in high-skill occupations, compared to the White third-plus generation. If all groups had exactly the same demographic and educational characteristics, most second generation minority groups would be very similar to the White third-plus generation with respect to their chances of working in high-skill occupations.

This analysis helps us understand the factors underlying the occupational scores of visible-minority second-generation groups compared to the White third-plus generation. The occupational scores under discussion differ from the percentage in high-skill occupations. The scores represent averages along a distribution of socioeconomic scores calculated for the 30 broad occupational groups available in the 2011 National Household Survey Microdata File on Individuals. If one group has a higher average score than another group, members of the first group work in occupations that on average are characterized by higher education and earnings compared with all other occupations. Because the percentages and averages of distributions are different measures, the results for occupational scores will not exactly replicate what was found above for the percentages holding high-skill occupations. However, the findings still confirm the importance of educational attainment in explaining why some groups have higher scores than others do.

How do we know this? The first column of Table 5.2 (see page 74) shows that Latin American and Black visible-minority members of the second generation have the lowest average occupational scores while the Chinese and South Asians have the highest scores. The second column expresses these numbers as deviations from the average score of 55 for the White third-plus generation. Here the conclusion is slightly more nuanced. The average occupational scores for the second generation who are Arab or Black are within one or two points of the score for the White third-plus generation—too small to be statistically significant. However, the occupational score for members of the Latin American second generation is nearly six points lower than that of the White third-plus generation, indicating that the Latin American second generation on average holds significantly lower ranked occupations. Conversely, occupational scores are higher for other visible-minority groups, indicating that they tend to be in occupations that have combined education and earnings that are higher than observed for the White third-plus generation.

Table 5.2. Regression of Average Occupational Score on Demographic and Educational Predictors,[a] Canada, 2011

	Actual Value	Model 1 Actual Value	Model 2 Demographic Characteristics[b]	Model 3 Demographic & Educational Characteristics[c]
Group		Deviations from the White 3rd-plus Generation		
White, 3rd+ generation (rg)	55.2			
Arab, 2nd generation	57.4	2.2	-0.2	-4.2**
Black, 2nd generation	54.0	-1.2	-3.2***	-1.7**
Chinese, 2nd generation	67.7	12.5***	10.9***	1.2*
Filipino, 2nd generation	60.4	5.2***	2.6*	-0.9
Other Southeast Asian, 2nd generation	60.8	5.5**	4.4**	-0.4
South Asian, 2nd generation	65.0	9.8***	7.9***	1.4*
Latin American, 2nd generation	49.6	-5.6**	-8.0***	-4.0**
Other visible minority, 2nd generation	60.5	5.3***	2.8**	-0.4
White, 2nd generation	58.2	3.0***	1.5***	0.0

*p<0.05; **p<0.01; ***p<0.001
rg = reference group
(a) For people age 25-39, not in school and with an occupation code.
(b) Demographic characteristics include sex, age, city of residence, province of residence, and marital status.
(c) Educational characteristics include highest educational level attained and field of study.

Note: Significance levels are for the logits produced from logistic regression using the indicator method.

Source: Computed from Statistics Canada, 2011 National Household Survey Public Use Microdata File on Individuals.

Table 5.2, column 3, shows the size of the deviations from the White third-plus generation that would exist for the visible-minority second generation if all groups were alike in their demographic characteristics. The results indicate that differences between the second and third-plus generations in demographic characteristics explain part of the occupational score differences between groups. The deviations in scores between the second generation groups and the White third-plus generation would decrease but not disappear if everyone were alike in terms of the distributions for sex age, marital status, city or residence, and province of residence. Much of the influence is due to geographical location—if the second generation were more like the third-plus generation in where they live, they would lose part of their access to higher scoring occupations simply because the range and types of occupations in large cities like Toronto and Vancouver are dissimilar from those in places like Kawartha Lakes or Rimouski. After taking these geographical and demographic characteristics into account, the Latin American second generation has an average occupational score nearly 8 points lower and the score for the Black second generation has a score more than 3 points lower than that observed for the White third-plus generation.

Table 5.2, column 4 compares the groups assuming they have the same demographic *and* educational characteristics. The deviations in column 4 are in general smaller and more often statistically not significant than those in column 3, suggesting that educational characteristics account for much of the between-group variation in occupational scores. If all groups were alike with respect to their demographic and educational characteristics, the gap in average occupational scores between the White third-plus generation and the Chinese and South Asian second generations would remain significant, very small, and in favour of the Chinese and South Asians. The gap between the White third-plus generation and the Filipino and Other Southeast Asian second generations would not be statistically significant. However, Arab, Black, and Latin American second generations would have significantly lower average occupational scores than the White third-plus generation does. These last results indicate that the original similarity observed in occupational scores between the Arab and Black second generation and the White third-plus generation largely reflect the more advantageous demographic and educational characteristics of these two second generation groups. Absent these characteristics, the average occupational scores would be lower than those of the White third-generation.

Back to the Future

Results of the 2011 National Household Survey tell us that second-generation Canadians—those born in Canada but with one or more foreign-born parents—tend to have high educational levels, and that their occupational profiles generally reflect those high educational attainments. In the age cohort that is the focus of this chapter (age 25-39), variation exists among the visible-minority second generations in regard to education, the incidence of holding high-skill occupations and in average occupational scores. My analysis shows that most visible-minority second-generation groups benefit from living disproportionately in large cities and from other demographic characteristics and that their occupational profiles also reflect their usually higher levels of education compared to the White third-plus generation. Said differently, the higher occupational profiles of many visible-minority second-generation groups largely reflect their demographic characteristics and their educational attainment. That said, not everyone shares the same outcomes. The Latin American second generation especially has low levels of education and occupational characteristics, well below those observed for the White third-plus generation.

Like many other visible minority labels, "Latin American" is a composite label, covering groups of diverse origin with different migration histories and different modes of entry (refugees, economic migrants, and so on). Future research on the socioeconomic integration of the second generation will benefit from greater attention to the specific groups that comprise the broad visible-minority categories (Boyd and Tian 2016). Additionally, the findings presented here are merely the tip of the knowledge iceberg for educational and occupational outcomes. What is it about education that is associated with labour market outcomes and what determines level of attainment? This chapter emphasized the roles played by parents and other family of origin characteristics but quality of schooling, peer groups, supplemental educational programs, and scholarships are also factors. An occupation is a job that occurs in a work environment; the type and size of firms and their recruitment and promotion practices, including discrimination, also influence occupational careers over the life cycle (Dechief and Oreopoulos 2012). Data that go beyond census-type questions are needed to further illuminate the socio-economic integration of the second generation in Canada.

The second generation discussed here was born to migrants who arrived in Canada by the mid-1980s. Many more immigrants have arrived since then, increasingly from areas other than Europe and the United States. Many of their children are still in school. However, by 2026 these immigrants and the rest of the second generation could represent nearly half of all Canadians (Morency, Malenfan, and MacIsaac 2017). These demographics indicate the importance of future research into the socio-economic integration of the second generation, with new attention given to the next cohorts that are reaching adulthood.

References

Abada, Teresa and Sylvia Lin. 2014. "Labour market outcomes of the children of immigrants in Ontario." *Canadian Studies in Population* 41(1-2): 78-96.

Abada, Teresa, Feng Hou and Bali Ram. 2009. "Ethnic differences in educational attainment among the children of Canadian immigrants." *Canadian Journal of Sociology* 34(1): 1-30.

Abada Teresa and Eric Y. Tenkorang. 2009. "Pursuit of university education among the children of immigrants in Canada: The roles of parental human capital and social capital." *Journal of Youth Studies* 12(2): 185-207.

Aydemir, Abdurrahman, Wen-Hao Chen, and Miles Corak. 2009. "Intergenerational earnings mobility among the children of Canadian immigrants." *Review of Economics and Statistics* 91(2): 377-97.

_____, _____ and _____. 2013. "Intergenerational education mobility among the children of Canadian immigrants." *Canadian Public Policy* 39(S1): S107-22.

Abdurrahman, Aydemir and Arthur Sweetman. 2008. "First- and second-generation immigrant attainment and labor market outcomes: A comparison of the United States and Canada." *Research in Labor Economics* 27: 215–270. (Special Issue: Immigration: Trends, Consequences and Prospects for the United States.)

Bonikowska, Aneta. 2007. "Explaining the education gap between children of immigrants and the native born: Allocation of human capital investments in immigrant families." Unpublished Paper. https://pdfs.semanticscholar.org/8a9d/d34239d300cb7c9616b4ed92f169254701fb.pdf.

Boyd, Monica. 2002. "Educational attainments of immigrant offspring: Success or segmented assimilation?" *International Migration Review* 36(4): 1037-1060.

_____. 2008a. "A socioeconomic scale for Canada: Measuring occupational status from the census." *Canadian Review of Sociology* 45(1): 51-91.

_____. 2008b. "Variations in socio-economic outcomes of second generation young adults." *Canadian Diversity* 6(2): 20-24.

_____. 2009. "Social origins and the educational and occupational achievements of the 1.5 and second generations." *Canadian Review of Sociology* 46(4): 339-69.

_____. 2014. "Recruiting high skill labour in North America: Policies, outcomes and futures." *International Migration* 52(3): 40-54.

_____. 2017. "Race and the labour market integration of second generation young adults." In Patrizia Albanese, Lorne Tepperman, and Emily Alexander, eds. *Reading Sociology*. Toronto: Oxford University Press.

Boyd, Monica and Naomi Alboim. 2012. "Managing international migration: The Canadian case." Pp. 123050 in Dan Rodríguez-García, ed. *Managing Immigration and Diversity in Canada: A Transatlantic Dialogue in the New Age of Migration*. Montreal and Kingston: McGill-Queen's University Press.

Boyd, Monica and Elizabeth Grieco. 1998. "Triumphant transitions: Socioeconomic achievements of the second generation in Canada." *International Migration Review* 22(4): 857-76.

Boyd, Monica, James Junmin Jeong, and Siyue Tian. 2014. "Does education lift all boats? The occupational and earnings attainments of Asian 1.5 and second generations." Presented in the "Asians and Asian Americans," regular session of the annual meeting of the American Sociological Association, August 16-19, San Francisco.

Boyd, Monica and Siyue Tian. 2016. "Educational and labor market attainments of the 1.5- and second-generation children of East Asian immigrants in Canada." *American Behavioral Scientist* 60(5-6): 705-29.

Boyd, Monica and Michael Vickers. 2016. "The ebb and flow of immigration in Canada." Pp. 155-72 in Edward Grabb, Jeffrey G. Reitz, and Monica Hwang, eds. *Social Inequality in Canada: Dimensions of Disadvantage*, 6th ed. Toronto: Oxford University Press.

Boyd, Monica, J. Goyder, F.E. Jones, H.A. McRoberts, P. Pineo, and J. Porter. 1985.

Ascription and Achievement: Studies in Mobility and Status Attainment. Ottawa: Carleton University Press.

Chen, Wen-Hao and Feng Hou. 2016. "Diversity in intergenerational education mobility and in labour market returns to education among the second generation of immigrants." Unpublished Paper, September. Statistics Canada: Social Analysis and Modeling Division.

Childs, Stephen, Ross Finnie, and Richard E. Mueller. 2015. "Why do so many children of immigrants attend university? Evidence for Canada." *Journal of International Migration & Integration* 18(1): 1-28.

Dechief, Diane and Philip Oreopoulos. 2012. "Why do some employers prefer to interview Matthew but not Samir? New evidence from Toronto, Montreal and Vancouver." Canadian Labour Market and Skills Researcher Network Working Paper No. 95. March. http://www.clsrn.econ.ubc.ca/workingpapers/CLSRN%20Working%20Paper%20no.%2095%20-%20Dechief%20and%20Oreopoulos.pdf.

Feliciano, Cynthia. 2005. "Does selective migration matter? Explaining ethnic disparities in educational attainment among immigrants' children." *International Migration Review* 39(4): 841-71.

Feliciano, Cynthia. 2006. "Beyond the family: The influence of premigration group status on the educational expectations of immigrants' children." *Sociology of Education* 79(4): 281-303.

Feliciano, Cynthia and Yader R. Lanuza. 2016. "The immigrant advantage in adolescent educational expectations." *International Migration Review* 50(3): 758–92.

Finnie, Ross and Richard E. Mueller. 2010. "They came, they saw, they enrolled: Access to post-secondary education by the children of Canadian immigrants." Pp. 191-216 in Ross Finnie, Marc Frenette, Richard E. Mueller, and Arthur Sweetman, eds. *Pursuing Higher Education in Canada: Economic, Social, and Policy Dimensions.* Montreal and Kingston: Queen's University Press.

Frenette, Marc and Rene Morissette. 2005. "Will they ever converge? Earnings of immigrant and Canadian-born workers over the last two decades." *International Migration Review* 39(1): 228-57.

Hirschman, Charles. 2016. *From High School to College: Gender, Immigrant Generation, and Race-Ethnicity.* New York: Russell Sage.

Hoe, Alice. 2012. "Explaining the educational gap among children from low-education families: Children of immigrants and the third-plus generation." MA thesis, Department of Sociology, University of Toronto.

Hou, Feng and Garnett Picot. 2016. "Changing immigrant characteristics and entry earnings." Analytical Studies Branch Research Paper Series No. 374. Ottawa: Statistics Canada. http://www.statcan.gc.ca/pub/11f0019m/11f0019m2016374-eng.pdf.

Ichou, Mathieu. 2014. "Who they were there: Immigrants' educational selectivity and their children's educational attainment." *European Sociological Review* 30(6): 750–65.

Jasso, Guillermina. 2011. "Migration and stratification." *Social Science Research* 40(5): 1292–1336.

Kao, Grace and Marta Tienda. 1995. "Optimism and achievement: The educational performance of immigrant youth." *Social Science Quarterly* 74(1): 1-19.

Kelly, Philip. 2014. "Understanding intergenerational social mobility: Filipino youth in Canada." IRPP Study #45. Montreal: Institute for Research on Public Policy. http://irpp.org/wp-content/uploads/assets/research/diversity-immigration-and-integration/filipino-youth/kelly-feb-2014.pdf.

Lee, Jennifer and Min Zhou. 2015. *The Asian American Achievement Paradox.* New York: Russell Sage.

Maheux, Hélène and René Houle. 2016. "150 years of immigration in Canada." Ottawa: Statistics Canada. http://www.statcan.gc.ca/pub/11-630-x/11-630-x2016006-eng.htm.

Morency, Jean-Dominique, Éric Caron Malenfant, and Samuel MacIsaac. 2017.

Immigration and Diversity: Population Projections for Canada and its Regions, 2011 to 2036. Ottawa: Statistics Canada. Catalogue No.91-551-X. http://www.statcan.gc.ca/pub/91-551-x/91-551-x2017001-eng.htm.
Picot, Garnett. 2004. "The deteriorating economic welfare of Canadian immigrants." *Canadian Journal of Urban Research* 13(1): 25-46.
Picot, Garnett and Feng Hou. 2010. "Preparing for success in Canada and the United States: The determinants of educational attainment among the children of immigrants." Canadian Labour Market and Skills Researcher Network (CLMSR) Working Paper No. 59. www.clsrn.econ.ubc.ca/workingpapers/CLSRN.
_____ and _____. 2013. "Why immigration matters for university participation: A comparison of Canada and Switzerland." *International Migration Review* 47(3): 612-42.
Picot, Garnett and Arthur Sweetman. 2005. "The deteriorating economic welfare of immigrants and possible causes: Update 2005." Research Paper Series No. 262. Ottawa: Statistics Canada, Analytical Studies Branch. http://www.statcan.gc.ca/pub/11f0019m/11f0019m2005262-eng.pdf.
Quillian, Lincoln. 2006. "New approaches to understanding racial prejudice and discrimination." *Annual Review of Sociology* 32(1): 299-328.
Reitz, Jeffrey G., Heather Zhang, and Naoko Hawkins. 2011. "Comparisons of the success of racial minority immigrant offspring in the United States, Canada and Australia." *Social Science Research* 40(4): 1051-66.
Statistics Canada. n.d. "National Occupational Classification 2011." http://www.statcan.gc.ca/eng/subjects/standard/noc/2011/index.
Sweet, Robert, Paul Anisef, Rob Brown, David Walters, and Kelli Phythian. 2009. "Post-high school pathways of immigrant youth." Final Report to Higher Education Quality Council of Ontario (HEQCO). http://www.heqco.ca/en-ca/Research/ResPub/Pages/Post-High-School-Pathways-of-Immigrant-Youth.aspx.
Taylor, Alison and Harvey Krahn. 2005. "Aiming high: Educational aspirations of visible minority immigrant youth." *Canadian Social Trends* 79: 8-12.

CHAPTER SIX
Immigration, Precarious Noncitizenship, and the Changing Landscape of Work[1]

Patricia Landolt

The Growth of Precarious Noncitizenship
Dramatic shifts in the volume and character of global migration movements compel us to look anew at legal status and noncitizenship as determinants of well-being, mobility and immobility, inequality, and stratification. The size of the global precarious noncitizen population is sobering. In 2015, almost 244 million people lived outside of their country of birth (Skeldon 2013), 20.2 million people were refugees or living in refugee-like situations (United Nations High Commission for Refugees 2015), and the number of international students worldwide had risen above 5 million (Education 2015). There were an estimated 150.3 million migrant workers (International Labour Organization 2015), and 50 million irregular migrants worldwide (International Organization for Migration 2014).

States have responded to global migration flows and refugee crises by creating many different and changing noncitizen legal status categories, restricting access to citizenship, eroding the rights of noncitizens and citizens, and developing extralegal systems for detaining and deporting people who have unclear citizenship rights. Running counter to this global lockdown, substantive citizenship and claims making by noncitizens are proliferating. In Canada, the relationship between noncitizenship, immobility, and inequality is evident in two overlapping arenas of social life (Landolt and Goldring 2016).

First, precarious noncitizenship is now a crosscutting feature of the im-

[1]. This paper draws on research and publications development through an extended research collaboration with Professor Luin Goldring, Department of Sociology, York University.

migration system. An overhaul of immigration policy has expanded the flow of temporary noncitizen migration to Canada and changed the relationship between the flow of temporary migrant noncitizens with no clear path to citizenship and the flow of permanent immigrants en route to citizenship (Goldring and Landolt 2012). Precarious noncitizens are at the interstice of this policy shift; they are migrants in myriad legal status categories who spend extended periods living and working in Canada with only partial rights and entitlements. Their presence in Canada as well as their access to labour markets and state entitlements are temporary, incomplete, and predicated on fulfilling formal requirements and discretionary conditions set by the state and non-state actors. Employers are the most important non-state actor in this mediated condition. Ultimately, precarious noncitizens' failure to meet conditions set by employers and the state results in loss of access to work and deportation (Goldring and Landolt 2013).

Second, precarious noncitizenship now mediates the relationship between immigration, work, and labour markets. Mediation occurs at several contact points between a revamped immigration system that favours precarious temporary migration over permanent immigration and the organization of workplaces and structure of regional labour markets. Precarious noncitizenship places limits on the ability of workers to claim and exercise their rights (Nakache and Kinoshita 2010). People who spend extended periods living and working in Canada as precarious noncitizens have troubled post-regularization economic experiences. Transition to permanent residence does not remove the corrosive impact of previous noncitizenship (Goldring and Landolt 2011; Landolt and Goldring 2013a). Further, research finds that the presence of precarious noncitizens with hampered or less-than-full rights at work exerts downward pressure on the regulatory and normative floor defining an acceptable employment relation and work conditions (Bernhardt, Boushey, Dresser, and Tilly 2008; Gammage 2008). As such, mixed legal status workplaces become sites for the formal and substantive erosion of rights of all workers, regardless of citizenship. Finally, from the perspective of labour markets, the presence of precarious noncitizen workers in strategic sites and sectors of the economy may erode labour market regulations and wage rates overall.

My analysis of precarious noncitizenship as a new fault line of social inequality in Canadian society is organized in four sections. I first define the concept of precarious noncitizenship and discuss two key features of vulnerability that characterize the condition of noncitizen workers: deportability and unfree labour. Second, I discuss recent changes in immigration policy that are relevant to precarious noncitizenship. Third, I use government data, original research, and secondary sources to track the impact of policy change on immigration trends and the economic geography of noncitizenship. I consider the intended and unintended consequences of policy and identify important gaps in data and blind spots in analysis. Fourth, I draw on interviews with precarious noncitizens to examine how the conditions of deportability and unfree labour influence work experience. I also use primary and secondary data sources to offer a preliminary analysis of the labour market outcomes of workers who transition from precarious noncitizenship to the secure legal status of permanent residence.

The Character of Precarious Noncitizenship

Both citizenship and noncitizenship are characterized by formal, legal elements and substantive conditions that emerge in the practice of citizenship and noncitizenship (Bloemraad, Korteweg, and Yurdakul 2008; Bosniak 2000; Yuval-Davis 1997). As discrete legal status categories, citizenship and noncitizenship are mirror opposites; the former denotes rights and responsibilities, the latter their absence (Bosniak 1994). In practice, the exercise and experience of citizenship and noncitizenship by individuals and groups is uneven (Sharma 2006). Both intersect with social location (Yuval-Davis 1997), spatiality and scale (Painter and Philo 1995) and the discretionary power of state agents to interpret and enforce regulations in a variable fashion (Alpes and Spire 2014).

Noncitizen precarious legal status categories specify the formal bases regulating how long and under what restrictions people can remain in a foreign country and the formal conditions governing their access to labour markets and social citizenship, particularly access to state entitlements such as education and healthcare. Noncitizens have precarious legal status if their situation in a country is marked by the absence of a permanent right to remain in a national territory, lack of permanent work authorization, limited or no access to social citizenship rights and entitlements, and/or deportability (Goldring, Berinstein, and Bernhard 2009). Deportability is a condition in which the state has the sovereign right to remove a person from the national territory forcibly; the power of this right lies in the fact that, although rarely exercised, it is always a possibility that hangs over the deportable migrant with profound and chilling effect (De Genova 2002; Villegas 2012). The legal conditions of precarious noncitizenship also establish possibilities for, and formal pathways of, legal status transitions. Depending on the legal status category of entry, changing policies, and migrant relations with intermediaries, precarious noncitizens may inhabit a status category with a clear and speedy pathway to naturalization and citizenship, blocked access to citizenship, lateral movement within temporary legal status categories, or illegalization (Goldring and Landolt 2013; Landolt and Goldring 2013b; Vickstrom 2014).

Substantively, precarious noncitizenship is relational, dynamic, uneven and unequal in experience and outcome. Individuals and institutions negotiate the formal systems and substantive practices through which noncitizens are conferred or denied rights to remain in a country and access entitlements. Noncitizens may choose to make claims to formal and substantive rights. The individuals and institutions with which they interact, informed by narratives of deservingness and moral worthiness, make discretionary decisions about these claims and rights that may encourage or discourage further claims-making. There is a high degree of indeterminacy and contingency in experiences and legal status trajectories of precarious noncitizenship (Landolt and Goldring 2016).

In Canada, the population of precarious legal status noncitizens includes but is not limited to all categories of authorized temporary migrants such as international students and their partners and foreign-born children; refugee claimants; parents and grandparents in Canada on a "super visa;" and temporary migrant workers, including migrants in the Temporary Foreign Worker Program, the Seasonal Agricultural Worker Program, and the Live-In Caregiver Program. It also includes non-status migrants who may become and remain unauthorized for a few months or many years as a result of overstaying an expired tourist visa, going underground once their asylum application is denied, or entering Canada undetected.

The condition of unfree labour mediates the formal and substantive practices of precarious noncitizens' experiences in the workplace. Unfree workers cannot circulate in the labour market, are required to work as the need arises and against their will by the threat of destitution, detention, deportation, violence, lawful compulsion or extreme hardship to themselves or members of their family (Basok 2002; Fudge and Strauss 2013; Lewis, Dwyer, Hodkinson, and Waite 2015; Miles 1982). Temporary migrant workers who are in Canada on a "tied visa" are a clear case of unfree labour. This category includes workers in the Temporary Foreign Worker Program, the Seasonal Agricultural Workers Program, and the Live-In Caregiver Program. All of these programs restrict migrant workers' presence and right to work in Canada to a visa and work permit that is held by the employer. Temporary migrants in other legal status categories may be able to circulate more freely in the labour market and their continued presence in Canada may not be tied to the maintenance of a relationship with a fixed employer. However, these temporary migrant workers are often precluded from exiting unfree labour because of indebtedness, wage withholding, and/or financial need (Landolt and Goldring 2013a).

Policy Changes and the Restructuring of the Immigration System

The federal government has always played an important role in organizing and managing the Canadian immigration system. It has used a mix of immigration and labour market policies to balance the tension between long-term immigration for population growth and short-term migration for labour supply.

Immigration policy in particular has been used to design a two-track system for migrant selection, settlement, and removal (Goldring and Landolt 2012; Sharma 2006). One track is for temporary migrants who are authorized to work and remain in Canada for a fixed period; have significant restrictions on where they can work and whether they can bring their family members; and face probationary conditions for establishing a route to citizenship. Examples include workers from China who came to Canada to work on the railway and in mining in the 1900s, Caribbean women who came to work as domestics in the 1950s, and Mexican and Jamaican workers who started migrating for seasonal agricultural work in the 1970s (Bakan and Stasiulis 1997; Basok 2002; Sharma 2006). The other, permanent track has selected immigrants for long-term settlement and eventual citizenship. Over time, the criteria for selection have changed—from race and country of origin to a focus on individual traits such as education, occupational skills, employment prospects, age, proficiency in English and French, and personal character (Elrick 2016).

Beginning in the 1990s, the declining economic fortunes of immigrants and rapid changes in the global economy prompted a reformulation of the balance between long- and short-term economic and demographic priorities. To a degree, concern for social citizenship and Canada's international humanitarian obligations were lost in the shuffle. The focus of political debate became the relationship between immigrant selection, the labour market prospects or "performance" of newcomers, and the creation of a flexible workforce as defined by the needs of employers (Alboim and Cohl 2012; Reitz 2014).

The federal government made three types of policy changes related to immigration management. First, the temporary migration track was overhauled. In 2002, the Non-Immigrant Employment Authorization Program, in place since 1973 to manage temporary migration, was retooled as the Low-Skill Pilot Project. The Low-Skill Pilot Project allowed companies in Canada to recruit low skill temporary migrant workers. Over time, the list of occupations that qualified for the program grew. In 2012, the program was renamed the Temporary Foreign Worker Program. An Accelerated Labour Market Opinion targeting skilled workers was then introduced. The latter policy allowed employers to pay workers 15 percent less than the recognized market rate but was suspended in 2013. However, the Temporary Foreign Worker Program remains in place.

The Temporary Foreign Worker Program facilitates short-term, labour-market flexibility for employers and makes employers a critical intermediary in precarious noncitizen workers' ability to stay and to work in Canada. Temporary foreign workers are in

Canada on tied work visas, meaning they can work only for the company or employer who holds their visa and for the time specified by the work permit. Work permit renewals, when allowed by an immigration program stream, require employer intermediation. If the employer wishes to dispose of the worker for any reason—production slowdowns, disagreements, worker injury, and so on—the visa can be terminated and the worker removed from the country. Further, temporary foreign workers cannot change their employer or be formally reassigned to work that is at a different skill level classification than the one with which they entered Canada. These restrictions are in place regardless of the actual education and skills of the worker (Fudge and MacPhail 2009).

Expansion of the temporary migration track was not limited to the Temporary Foreign Worker Program. Many other precarious noncitizens who were in Canada for long periods were issued work permits. Other, longstanding temporary migrant worker programs, such as the Seasonal Agriculture Workers Program and the Live-in Caregiver Program, continued to function alongside the Temporary Foreign Worker Program and grow. A variety of temporary migrants were issued closed and/or open work permits that were not restricted to a specific employer or skill classification. They included spouses of temporary migrant workers in different programs and streams, refugee claimants, and international students.

Parallel to changes in temporary migration were slower but equally significant shifts in the permanent immigration track. Changes in the system for direct entry of permanent residents through the Federal Skilled Worker Program began in the 1990s and were formalized in the 2002 Immigration and Refugee Protection Act. The Federal Skilled Worker Program began to reward more points for general human capital, putting a premium on education, experience, and language ability rather than proficiency in specific occupations (Ferrer, Picot, and Riddell 2014). The Canadian Immigrant Investor Program, which enabled qualified investors to obtain permanent resident status in Canada, was expanded, but then terminated in 2014. Changes to the Federal Skilled Worker Program culminated in the creation of the Express Entry system in 2014. This is a two-step skilled immigrant selection system in which all applicants are screened to enter the pool and then ranked against each other and invited to apply for permanent residency in accordance with their rank. The new system allows employers to be matched with qualified candidates through the federal government's job bank.

Adjustments were made in the relationship between the temporary and permanent migration tracks and in the role of non-state intermediaries in managing the relationship. The Immigration and Refugee Protection Act created new immigration programs, such as the Canadian Experience Class and the Provincial Nominee Program. They enabled select categories of temporary migrants to transition from temporary to permanent residence status. For example, the Canadian Experience Class allowed some skilled categories of temporary foreign workers with Canadian work experience and international students who had a Canadian degree and at least one year of Canadian work experience to apply to transfer their temporary resident status to permanent status without leaving the country. The Provincial Nominee Program sought to locate more immigrants outside of the three major cities of immigrant reception (Toronto, Montreal, and Vancouver) and to meet the workforce needs of local employers (Seidle 2013). Many immigrants entering via the Provincial Nominee Program have pre-arranged jobs. The short-term needs of employers are thus embedded in the selection process (Ferrer, Picot, and Riddell 2014). Employers again play an important role as intermediaries in the transition from temporary to permanent migration.

Policy Impacts: Evidence of Expected and Unexpected Trends

Let us now consider the impact of immigration policy overhauls, first by focusing on immigration flows and looking for evidence of change in temporary and permanent immigration trends and in the relationship between them. Let us then examine the economic geography of the two-track, two-step immigration system to consider changes in the sectoral and geographic distribution of temporary migrant workers across regional labour markets.

IMMIGRATION TRENDS, 1980s–2000s

Figure 6.1 (on the next page) shows that, since the mid-1980s, temporary migration has almost consistently outpaced permanent immigration. Moreover, the gap between temporary and permanent immigration has grown markedly since the mid-2000s. In 1983, the first year for which reliable data exists, there were 90,000 permanent entries and 200,000 temporary entries. Through the 1990s, temporary and permanent entries hovered around 220,000 each. In the 2000s, permanent immigrant entries levelled off and temporary entries increased rapidly. In 2012, there were more than 421,000 temporary entries, an increase of 109 percent since 1993.

Figure 6.2 (also on the next page) shows the stock (accumulated total) and flow (annual total) of authorized temporary migrants in Canada between 1983 and 2012. The "average" line tracks the mean number of stock and flow migrants by year. Note the near-steady increase in the size of the temporary migrant population (stock plus flow)—a growth of 236 percent between 1983 and 2012 to a total of nearly 1.1 million people. Note also the more or less steady increase in the ratio of stock to flow from 0.61 in 1983 to 1.59 in 2012. This trend suggests that temporary migrants have become a demographic fixture rather than a passing feature of Canadian society (Michalowski 1993).

A breakdown of the different program types and legal status categories that made up temporary migration in Canada between 1983 and 2012 (not shown here) indicates that the types of temporary migration that have experienced the greatest growth are workers and international students. The number of refugee and "other humanitarian" claimants increased substantially in the late 1980s and early 1990s but the number of refugee claimants has hardly budged since then while "other humanitarian" claimants have dropped to near zero.

Figure 6.3 (p. 91) provides evidence of the changing relationship between the temporary and permanent migration tracks. It presents data on the legal status composition of the population granted permanent residence from 2002 to 2012. The data show that the total permanent-resident population has remained nearly constant. It also shows that there has been a steady increase in the proportion of migrants who transition from a temporary migrant cat-

Figure 6.1. Permanent and Temporary Immigrants, 1983-2012

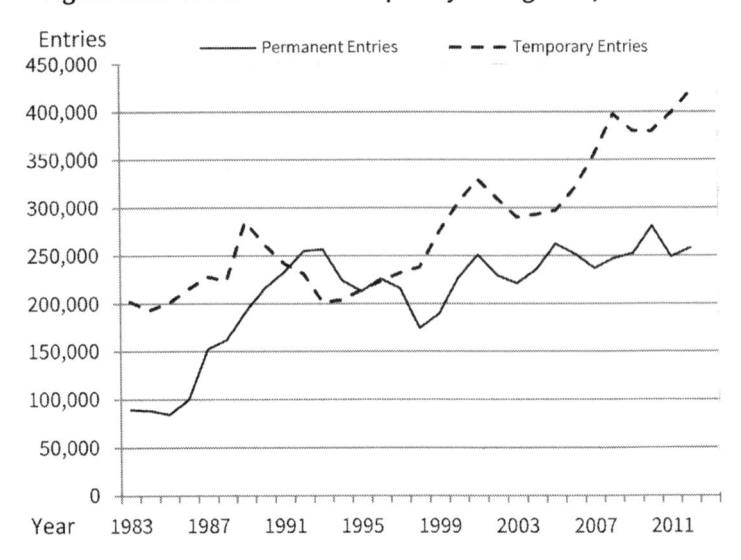

Source: Citizenship and Immigration Canada (2008; 2012)

Figure 6.2. Temporary Migration Stock and Flow, 1983-2012

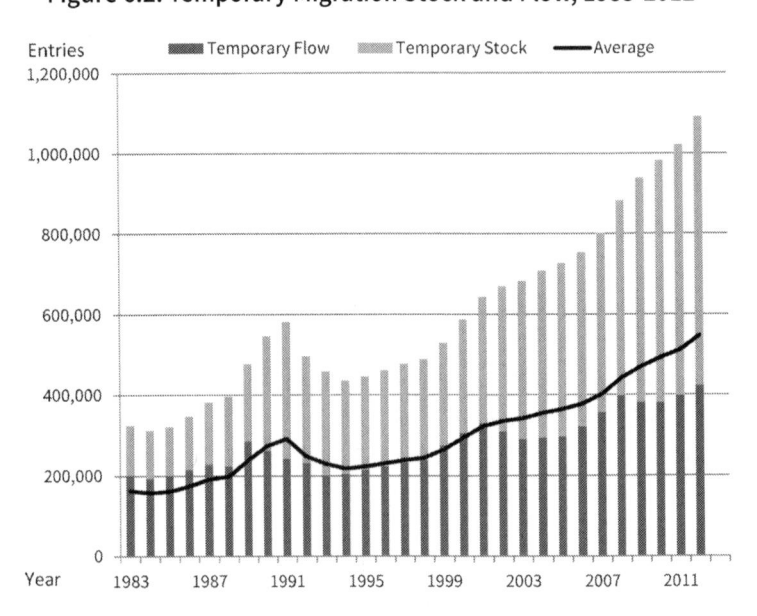

Source: Citizenship and Immigration Canada (2008; 2012).

90 *Immigration and the Future of Canadian Society*

Figure 6.3. Types of Permanent Immigrants, 2003-2012

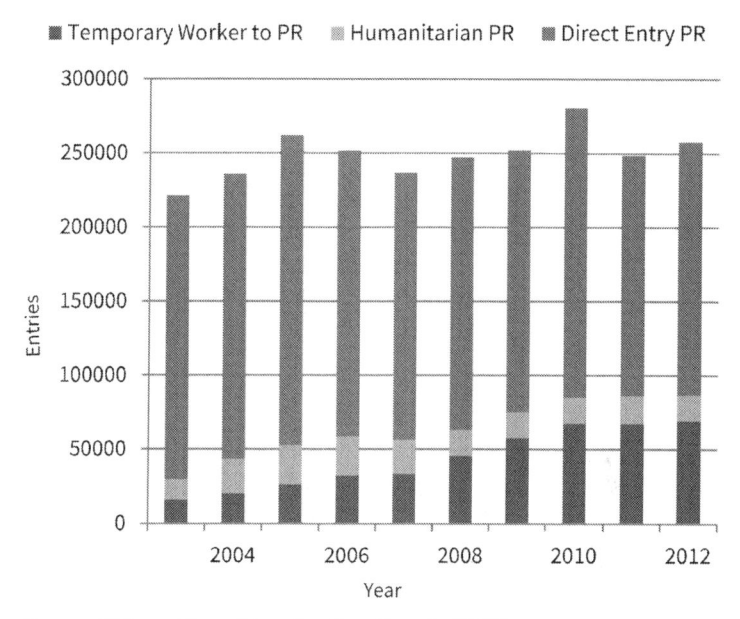

■ Temporary Worker to PR   ■ Humanitarian PR   ■ Direct Entry PR

Source: Citizenship and Immigration Canada (2012).

egory to permanent residence. In 2003, nearly 30,000 people—13.3 percent of those granted permanent residence—transitioned from a temporary category. In 2012, the comparable numbers swelled to nearly 87,000 and 50.8 percent.

Significant gaps exist in government data. For example, data on legal status transitions within temporary migrant categories is limited. Golding (2014) analyzed legal status transitions using existing administrative data. She found a substantial number of temporary migrants making lateral moves across three broad legal status categories: international student, humanitarian, and temporary worker. The largest number of transitions is from international student to the foreign worker category. Government data do not capture the number of lateral moves that people make or the time they spend in Canada as precarious noncitizens before transitioning to the permanent immigration track. Nor do they show whether temporary migrants spend time without status or a work permit before transitioning to permanent residence.

To compensate for such gaps in the data, I draw on a survey conducted among Latin American and Caribbean immigrant workers in the greater Toronto area in 2006. Luin Goldring and I interviewed 300 immigrant workers using a mixed-methods survey. Since there was no sampling frame with which to construct a representative sample, we used a multi-step random sampling design to generate a study population of 300 respondents. We took steps to produce a quota sample that reflected recent immigration trends for the two groups. There were five selection criteria for potential respondents, including: born in Spanish-speaking Latin America or English-speaking Caribbean country; arrived in Canada after June, 1990, and before June, 2004; age at arrival between 14 and 45 years; currently employed, at least 20 hours per week for the last two months; and not a full-time university or college student. We did not establish requirements regarding legal status, occupation, sector, or terms of employment, as we did not want to sample on the dependent variables (precarious work and precarious legal status). The two-hour interview covered many topics, including reasons for migration, early settlement experience including early job search and work experience, respondents' employment trajectory over time, including strategies to change and improve work conditions and find better work, contact with institutions, and detailed questions to capture changes in legal status over time, including strategies and efforts to move toward more secure legal status.[2]

We found that the 106 people who entered Canada with precarious legal status had gone through 240 legal status transitions. In some cases, the legal status transition was toward more insecure status, at other times toward more secure status and a path to permanent residence. The timelines on transitions were also varied. Fifty-seven of the 300 respondents had spent between 3 and 5 years living and working in Toronto with precarious legal status before transitioning to permanent residence. Thirty-one respondents had worked without a permit between 4 and 6 years before transitioning to permanent residence (Landolt and Goldring 2013b). The survey points to a complex landscape of temporally extended and uncertain legal status transitions that do not neces-

---

2. The research was funded by a grant from the Social Sciences and Humanities Research Council of Canada. For more information on the project, including research briefs and the survey questionnaire see Cities Centre, University of Toronto, and York University (2009).

sarily correspond to the two-track, two-step immigration system laid out by federal policy.

A second gap in administrative data concerns the non-status population. The government does not collect migration exit data and therefore cannot track who leaves or stays in the country; once migrants lack official status they are off the radar. More than a decade ago, the non-status population was crudely estimated at 200,000 to 500,000 (Jimenez 2003; 2006).

In sum, analysis of multiple data sources confirms the expected impact of the policy overhaul and reveals some of its unintended and poorly understood consequences. Government administrative data confirm a rapid and substantial increase in the flow and stock of temporary migrant entrants to Canada. In contrast, the flow of permanent resident entries has remained flat. My analysis also substantiates the impact of the two-step policy framework on the relationship between temporary and permanent immigration. The two-step policy was designed to change the relationship between the two migration tracks. That it has done. A growing proportion of the permanent migration track is composed of individuals who live and work in Canada as precarious noncitizens prior to transitioning to the secure legal status of permanent residence.

Administrative data do not permit a complete analysis of the unexpected and less well understood consequences of the two-track, two-step immigration system. Lateral legal status transitions, that is, transitions within temporary migrant categories, are an important and unexpected feature of the new immigration system. It is rarely discussed and its implications for the long-term incorporation of migrants are seldom contemplated. How long people live and work in a state of precarious noncitizenship prior to achieving permanent residence is unknown, as is how many times they adjust their precarious legal status during this period. The data also reveal a gap in our knowledge about the non-status population, although the population of de facto residents living and working in Canada without legal status for extended periods is likely sizeable. Thus, the two-step, two-track immigration system is much more complex than proposed or expected by the federal policy framework (Goldring and Landolt 2012).

The Economic Geography of Precarious Noncitizenship

Three data sources can help us understand the economic geography of precarious noncitizenship. First, Table 6.1 presents data on the number and proportion of urban centres in each province that hosted temporary foreign workers in 2015-16. Temporary foreign workers enter Canada based on an employer Labour Market Impact Assessment request. Their presence and access to the labour market is conditional on their ongoing tied-visa-based employment by the employer who submitted the Labour Market Impact Assessment request. Table 6.1 shows that, in 2015-16, the proportional impact of temporary foreign workers was greatest in Prince Edward Island, Nova Scotia, and Alberta, where between 86 percent and 41 percent of urban centres hosted temporary foreign workers. The proportional impact was smallest in British Columbia, Ontario, and Quebec, where between 18 and 12 percent of urban centres hosted temporary foreign workers. Note, however, that these percentages do not refer to the absolute number of temporary foreign workers in each province.

In his analysis of the 2006 Canadian census, Thomas (2010) identified urban centres where 1 percent or more of all full time workers were non-permanent residents. The list includes one-industry towns specializing in a range of economic activities, such as Canmore, Brooks, and Wood Buffalo in Alberta; Brandon, Manitoba; and Yellowknife, Northwest Territories. More than 1 percent of the full-time paid labour force in Canada's immigrant gateway cities—Toronto, Vancouver, Montreal, and Calgary—were also non-permanent residents.

In addition, the 2006 census documents the diverse occupations and sectors in which temporary entrants worked full time. The list includes care workers, research and teaching assistants, retail sales workers and managers, low-end service workers such as cleaners, food-counter workers, truck drivers, physicians, and religious ministers (Thomas 2010).

Finally, a comparison of occupational classifications for temporary foreign workers, based on Labour Market Opinion data for 2005 and 2008, reveals a sectoral and occupational shift in the temporary migrant worker population recruited through this program (Foster 2012). In 2005, the top five non-live-in-caregiver occu

Table 6.1
Temporary Foreign Workers by Urban Area and Province/Territory, 2015-16

Province/Territory	Number of urban centres with TFWs*	Percent of urban centres with TFWs*
Newfoundland and Labrador	8	27
Prince Edward Island	6	86
Nova Scotia	16	43
New Brunswick	13	39
Quebec	29	12
Ontario	38	14
Manitoba	9	20
Saskatchewan	18	29
Alberta	45	41
British Columbia	18	18
Nunavut, Northwest Territories, Yukon	3	27

*Temporary Foreign Worker.
Source: Government of Canada (2016).

pations listed were musicians and singers, actors and comedians, producers, directors and related occupations, specialist physicians, and other technical occupations in motion pictures and broadcasting. By 2008, the top five included food counter attendants and kitchen helpers, cooks, construction trades helpers and labourers, light-duty cleaners, and musicians and singers. The transformation of the list is marked. Three of the top five occupational groupings in 2008 were classified as low-skill occupations and only one remains from the 2005 top-five list (Foster 2012).

In short, the immigration policy overhaul has had a marked impact on the economic geography of precarious noncitizenship. The data are fragmented and offer only a partial picture of the transformation that has occurred across regional labour markets and sectors. Nonetheless, it points to a sectoral, occupational, and geographic diffusion of precarious noncitizen workers into work and labour markets across the country.

Precarious Noncitizenship, Work, and Labour Markets

Evaluations of the impact of the two-track, two-step immigration system on work and labour markets are mixed. Sectoral lobbies, employers, and their advocates and supporters in government applaud Canada's immigration system as an effective way to calibrate the global migrant worker supply and local labour market demand. Unions and migrant rights activists offer troubling and negative evidence of the impact of temporary migration and probationary migration schemes on work and labour markets. Against this contentious backdrop, I consider the impact of the two-track, two-step immigration system and precarious noncitizenship from two perspectives: the work experience of precarious noncitizens and the labour market outcomes of migrant workers who transition from temporary to permanent status.

Precarious Noncitizen Work Experiences

Of the 300 migrant workers whom Luin Goldring and I interviewed in Toronto in 2006, 150 held a precarious legal status upon entry to Canada. Sixty percent of them had transitioned to secure legal status and acquired permanent residence at the time of the interview. Their experience helps to shed light on the ways in which legal status influences work experience. Our survey revealed two constants in their work experience: wage theft and labour market immobility.

All workers, regardless of race, gender, education, and English language proficiency, experienced wage theft in their first year of work in Canada. A Colombian refugee claimant with a university education recounted:

> I think in my first year they stole from me maybe more than 60 percent of the times I worked; that it was a very precarious situation; that even though I spoke English—I spoke English when I arrived here—my lack of knowledge of the context, the surroundings.

He was dismayed that although he knew how to "handle himself" he experienced wage theft and could do little about it. Another respondent spoke of his powerlessness as follows:

> What happens is that as long as you don't have your work

permit and you work for cash, people abuse you. And, well, the truth is, yes, I was exploited a lot as well. I worked for very little money and I worked a lot of hours and a lot of those hours I was never paid....You would do the job just like any other person ... but because of the papers.... A person needs to eat, needs to buy stuff....You have to earn something.

A worker in the Live-in Caregiver program explained why she put up with an abusive employer in these words:

I told them all the time that they owed me money, and she was like, "Oh, we have three kids and we have the mortgage and that's all we can afford." And then this is the part that humiliated me: they would always make you feel because they sponsored you, they can just pay you $250, because she would say stuff like, "Remember we sponsored you and we're helping you in some way." So that probably they thought that they did that so they could pay me $250 and I shouldn't complain.

If precarious noncitizen workers are vulnerable to exploitation by employers and have little formal or substantive recourse, they also suffer labour immobility. Thus, workers on open work permits faced strict self-imposed limits on their ability to search for a new job and accepted low-end work to avoid prying questions from employers. As one of our respondents explained:

Prior to becoming a landed immigrant the only jobs—even though I knew better and I had skills and I knew that I could do all these things—but the only jobs I thought were within my range were cleaning people's houses, working in a factory or taking care of people's kids in their house, right. Um, those were also the jobs that you were less, um... intrusive, people weren't going to ask you about your personal business, they weren't going to ask you how you got there, can I see your proper insurance number.

Because of their need to secure a livelihood while remaining invisible to the authorities, workers without authorization to work in Canada talked about the need to take whatever bad employers offer. A non-status respondent explained her situation this way:

> People are willing to hire illegal people, but like the type of work, of course you have to take what you get, the type of employer, you take what you get....You don't have a wide variety, right, because you don't have a social [insurance] number, you're illegal, right. So when a job situation arises, it might not be much but you're willing to take it because, what else is there? You're not going to be able to go through unemployment insurance or anything so—social services, no, so you take what you get, because who's going to take care of you?

Although inability to change employers is imposed by the formal restrictions of the work permit and the immediate need to secure a livelihood, it is also driven by fear of jeopardizing the chance for legal status regularization and fear of detection and deportation. Deportability compounds the workplace vulnerabilities of unfree labour.

Legal Status Transitions and Work Outcomes

Federal immigration policy established new programs that permit precarious noncitizen workers to transition from temporary to permanent residence via the Canadian Experience Class and the Provincial Nominee Program. Other two-step legal status transitions that allow temporary migrants to apply for permanent residence have been in place for years. They include the people in the Live-in Caregiver Program, asylum seekers with a positive decision on their refugee application, and non-status migrants accepted via a Humanitarian and Compassionate Consideration. Myriad differences exist across these two-step tracks to permanent residence. What all of them have in common is that they involve temporary migrants working in Canada as precarious noncitizens prior to applying for permanent residence. Further, each of these two-step mechanisms involve intermediaries—employers, lawyers, and university administrators, among others—who play an important role in determining the eligibility and outcome of the application to transition to permanent residence.

The two-step immigration system is designed to ensure better labour market outcomes for permanent residents who are selected from a pool of migrants with labour market experience in Canada. Research on immigrant's post-regularization economic performance is in its infancy and findings are mixed. We know that skilled temporary foreign workers enjoy an earnings advantage over direct entry immigrants (Hou and Bonikowska 2016) but a major limitation of research on this population is the lack of data on pre-transition legal status trajectories and experience. I now review the evidence for a variety of legal status transition patterns and focus on post-transition work quality and skills mismatch.

In our survey of migrant workers in Toronto, Luin Goldring and I examined the post-transition labour market outcomes of migrants from a mix of temporary tracks including asylum seekers, Live-in Careworker Program workers, visa overstayers, and a small number of international students. It is important to recognize that this is not the intended population for the two-step system and we should not be surprised that regularization did not have a substantial positive effect on labour market outcomes (Goldring and Landolt 2011). However, the reasons for neutral and negative outcomes are worth noting. Across gender, educational levels, English language proficiency, and other indicators of human capital, we found that precarious employment conditions and general resource depletion experienced during years of living and working as precarious noncitizens had cumulative, negative, long-term effects. Regularization and the transition to permanent residence could not adjust for years of eroded conditions of livelihood. In our study, migrants who entered with temporary, precarious legal status, regardless of whether they were authorized to be in Canada and work here, spent long periods in bad jobs, worked for low-wages, had limited opportunities to improve the terms and conditions of their employment, and had few opportunities to invest in education as a stepping stone to better work. They also went into debt because of low income and wage theft and because of the cost associated with trying to regularize their legal status. These costs varied from a few thousand dollars to tens of thousands of dollars for lawyers and administrative fees (Landolt and Goldring 2013a).

Research on post-transition labour market outcomes of people in the Live-in Caregiver Program mirrors our findings. A survey of 657 permanent residents who entered Canada through the Live-in Caregiver Program found a significant post-regularization skills mismatch. Eighty-five percent of respondents had a university education but continued to work as caregivers three to five years out of the program (Tungohan et al. 2015). A qualitative study of 60 former Live-in Caregiver Program workers also found that respondents experienced permanent deskilling and did not go back to their pre-migration profession after regularization (Atanackovic and Bourgeault 2014). This research identifies various reasons for negative post-regularization outcomes, including limited social networks, racism, lack of credential recognition, losing recognition of previous training and skills, long and expensive upgrading processes, and limited eligibility and access to employment and settlement services prior to transition and after entry into permanent residence.

Finally, research on international students—often regarded by proponents as the jewel in the two-step, two-track immigration policy crown—reveals equally uncertain post-regularization outcomes. It is assumed that the international student experience (a Canadian degree, networks with fellow students, opportunities for off-campus employment, official language skills) will eradicate or at least reduce barriers to entry into the labour market faced by other migration streams (Chira 2013). The transition to permanent residence is meant to ensure that these highly skilled migrants will secure jobs commensurate with their skills and education. Research to date suggests that students are struggling to gain access to jobs and positive workplace experience. Students report facing discrimination and lack of employer trust as they transition into the labour market (Kim and Sondhi 2015). The research points to a lack of university-based settlement services for this population as one important factor.

Precarious Noncitizenship and Social Inequality

The rise of precarious noncitizenship as a central axis of the immigration system, work, and the labour market has three broad effects on the contours of social inequality in Canada.

First, migrants whose legal status trajectory includes a probationary period of employment with the curtailed rights and entitlements of noncitizenship experience the negative effects of their precarious status even after they achieve citizenship. In this way, precarious legal status becomes a new source of stratification with long-term, potentially inter-generational impact (Kelly 2014).

Second, the two-track system makes economic performance based on the evaluation and intermediation of employers an essential indicator of the right to access citizenship. The downloading of state authority regarding immigrant selection to employers prioritizes the interests of a narrow slice of society, one that is concerned first and foremost with individual profit, over those of other sectors. This downloaded authority to select future citizens contrasts sharply with the strong role of the federal government in selecting and vetting sponsored refugees. This variable and potentially inconsistent practice should be a subject of public debate.

Third, the new immigration system has the potential to introduce a democratic deficit into the operation of institutions in which precarious noncitizens are a significant presence (Lenard and Simeon 2012). Deportable noncitizen workers whose right to work in Canada is tied to an employer or who are focused on ensuring a successful transition to permanent immigration are not likely to make waves or demand rights at work—or anywhere else for that matter. To the extent that noncitizen workers are vulnerable and deportable, their presence weakens the floor on the formal and substantive rights of noncitizens and citizens alike.

References

Alboim, Naomi and Karen Cohl. 2012. "Shaping the Future: Canada's Rapidly Changing Immigration Policies." Toronto: Maytree Foundation.
Alpes, Maybritt Jill and Alexis Spire. 2014. "Dealing with Law in Migration Control: The Powers of Street-level Bureaucrats at French Consulates." *Social & Legal Studies* 23(2): 261-74.
Atanackovic, Jelena and Ivy Lynn Bourgeault. 2014. "Economic and Social Integration of Immigrant Live-in Caregivers in Canada." Ottawa: Institute for Research on Public Policy.
Bakan, Abigail B. and Daiva Stasiulis. 1997. *Not One of the Family: Foreign Domestic Workers in Canada*. Toronto: University of Toronto Press.
Basok, Tanya. 2002. *Tortillas and Tomatoes. Mexican Transmigrant Harvesters in Canada*. Kingston and Montreal: McGill-Queen's Press.
Bernhardt, Annette, Heather Boushey, Laura Dresser, and Charles Tilly. 2008. "The Gloves Off Economy: Workplace Standards at the Bottom of America's Labor Market." Champaign IL: Labor and Employment Relations Association.
Bloemraad, Irene, Anna Korteweg, and Gokce Yurdakul. 2008. "Citizenship and Immigration: Assimilation, Multiculturalism, and Challenges to the Nation-State." *Annual Review of Sociology* 34: 153-79.
Bosniak, Linda. 1994. "Membership, equality, and the difference that alienage makes." *New York University Law Review* 69(6): 1047-49.
_____. 2000. "Universal Citizenship and the Problem of Alienage." *Northwestern University Law Review* 94(3): 963-82.
Chira, Sinziana. 2013. "Dreaming Big, Coming Up Short: The challenging realities of international students and graduates in Atlantic Canada." Moncton NB: Atlantic Metropolis Centre.
Cities Centre, University of Toronto, and York University. 2009. "Immigrants in the Global Economy: Precarious Employment and the Transnational Dimensions of Economic Incorporation." http://www.yorku.ca/ine/research/index.html.
Citizenship and Immigration Canada. 2008. "Facts and Figures 2007: Immigration Overview, Permanent and Temporary Residents." Ottawa.
_____. 2012. "Preliminary Tables—Permanent and Temporary Residents, 2011." Ottawa.
De Genova, Nicholas. 2002. "Migrant "Illegality" and Deportability in Everyday Life." *Annual Review of Anthropology* 31:419-47.
Canadian Bureau for International Education. 2015. "2015 Annual Report." In *Facts & Figures: Canada's Performance and Potential in International Education*: Canadian Bureau for International Education. http://cbie.ca/media/facts-and-figures/
Elrick, Jennifer. 2016. "Family|Class: Race and Third-Order Immigration Policy in Post-War Canada." PhD dissertation, Department of Sociology, University of Toronto, Toronto.
Ferrer, Ana M., Garnett Picot, and William Craig Riddell. 2014. "New Directions in Immigration Policy: Canada's Evolving Approach to the Selection of Economic Immigrants." *International Migration Review* 48(3): 846-67.
Foster, Jason. 2012. "Making Temporary Permanent: The Silent Transformation of the Temporary Foreign Worker Program." *Just Labour* 19: 22-46.
Fudge, Judy and Fiona MacPhail. 2009. "The Temporary Foreign Worker Program in Canada: Low-Skilled Workers as an Extreme Form of Flexible Labour." *Comparative Labor Law and Policy Journal* 31(1): 101-39.
Fudge, Judy and Kendra Strauss. 2013. *Temporary Work, Agencies and Unfree Labour: Insecurity in the New World of Work*. New York & London: Routledge.
Gammage, Sarah. 2008. "Working on the Margins: Migration and Employment in the United States." Pp. 1-243 in *The Gloves-Off Economy: Workplace Standards at the Bottom of America's Labour Market*, A. Bernhardt, H. Boushey, L. Dresser, and C. Tilly, eds. Champaign IL: Labour and Employment Relations Association.
Goldring, Luin. 2014. "Resituating Temporariness as the Precarity and Condition-

ality of Non-citizenship." Pp. 218-254 in *Liberating Temporariness? Migration, Work and Citizenship in an Age of Insecurity*, L. Vosko, V. Preston, and R. Latham, eds. Montreal and Kingston: McGill-Queen's University Press.

Goldring, Luin, Carolina Berinstein, and Judith K. Bernhard. 2009. "Institutionalizing precarious migratory status in Canada." *Citizenship Studies* 13(3): 239-65.

Goldring, Luin and Patricia Landolt. 2011. "Caught in the Work-Citizenship Matrix: The lasting effects of precarious legal status on work for Toronto immigrants." *Globalizations* 8(3): 325-41.

_____ and _____. 2012. "The Impact of Precarious Legal Status on Immigrants' Economic Outcomes." Ottawa: Institute for Research in Public Policy.

_____ and _____. 2013. "The Conditionality of Legal Status and Rights: Conceptualizing Precarious Non-Citizenship in Canada." Pp. 3-29 in *Producing and Negotiating Non-citizenship: Precarious Legal Status in Canada*, L. Goldring and P. Landolt, eds. Toronto: University of Toronto Press.

Government of Canada. 2016. "Temporary Foreign Worker Program 2016 Q3." http://open.canada.ca/data/en/dataset/e8745429-21e7-4a73-b3f5-90a779b-78d1e?_ga=1.257621384.2035255981.1489374216.

Hou, Feng and Aneta Bonikowska. 2016. "Selections Before the Selection: Earnings Advantages of Immigrants Who Were Former Skilled Temporary Foreign Workers in Canada." *International Migration Review* doi:10.1111/imre.12310

International Labour Organization. 2015. "ILO Global estimates of migrant workers and migrant domestic workers: results and methodology." Geneva.

International Organization for Migration. 2014. "Global Migration Trends: An Overview." Geneva.

Jimenez, Marina. 2003. "Under the radar: 200,000 illegal immigrants toiling in Canada's underground economy." *Globe and Mail*: November 14, p. 6.

Jimenez, Marina. 2006. "Ottawa rules out amnesty for 200,000 illegal workers." *Globe and Mail* Oct. 27: p.A1

Kelly, Philip. 2014. "Understanding. Intergenerational. Social Mobility. Filipino Youth in Canada. Philip Kelly." Institute for Research in Public Policy, Ottawa.

Kim, Ann H. and Gunjan Sondhi. 2015. "Bridging the Literature on Education Migration: Synthesis Report for the Population Change and Lifecourse Strategic Knowledge Cluster." Toronto: York Centre for Asian Research.

Landolt, Patricia and Luin Goldring. 2013a. "The Social Production of Non-citizenship: The Consequences of Intersecting Trajectories of Precarious Legal Status and Precarious Work." Pp. 154-173 in *Producing and Negotiating Non-citizenship: Precarious Legal Status in Canada*, L. Goldring and P. Landolt, eds. Toronto: University of Toronto Press.

_____ and _____. 2013b. "Understanding the Canadian Immigration System: Linking together Tracked and Obscured Legal Status Transitions and Trajectories." Paper presented at the annual meetings of the Canadian Sociological Association. Victoria.

_____ and _____. 2016. "Assembling noncitizenship through the work of conditionality." *Citizenship Studies* 19(8): 853-69.

Lenard, Patti Tamara and Richard Simeon. 2012. *Imperfect Democracies: The Democratic Deficit in Canada and the United States*. Vancouver: University of Columbia Press.

Lewis, Hannah, Peter Dwyer, Stuart Hodkinson, and Louise Waite. 2015. "Hyper-precarious lives: Migrants, work and forced labour in the Global North." *Progress in Human Geography* 39(5): 580-600.

Michalowski, Margaret. 1993. "Redefining the concept of immigration in Canada." *Canadian Studies in Population* 20(1): 59-84.

Miles, Robert. 1982. *Racism and Migrant Labour*. London and Boston: Routledge & Kegan Paul.

Nakache, Delphine and Paula J. Kinoshita. 2010. "The Canadian Temporary Foreign Worker Program: Do Short-Term Economic Needs Prevail over Human Rights Concerns?" Ottawa: IRPP Study No. 5.

Painter, Joe and Chris Philo. 1995. "Spaces of Citizenship: An Introduction." *Political Geography* 14(2):107-20.
Reitz, Jeffrey. 2014. "Canada: New Initiatives and Approaches to Immigration and Nation Building." Pp. 88-116 in *Controlling Immigration: A Global Perspective*, J. Hollifield, P. Martin, and P. M. Orrenius, eds. Stanford CA: Stanford University Press.
Seidle, Leslie. 2013. "Canada's Provincial Nominee Immigration Programs: Securing Greater Policy Alignmnent." Ottawa: Institute for Research in Public Policy.
Sharma, Nandita. 2006. *Home Economics: Nationalism and the Making of "Migrant Workers" in Canada*. Toronto: University of Toronto Press.
Skeldon, Ronald. 2013. "Global Migration: Demographic Aspects and its Relevance for Development." New York: Department of Economic and Social Affairs, Population Division, United Nations.
Thomas, Derrick. 2010. "Foreign Nationals Working Temporarily in Canada." Ottawa: Statistics Canada.
Tungohan, Ethel, Rupa Banerjee, Wayne Chu, Petronila Cleto, Conely de Leon, Mila Garcia, Philip Kelly, Marco Luciano, Cynthia Palmaria, and Christopher Sorio. 2015. "After the Live-in Caregiver Program: Filipina Caregivers' Experiences of Graduated and Uneven Citizenship." *Canadian Ethnic Studies* 47(1): 87-105.
United Nations High Commission for Refugees. 2015. "Mid-Year Trends 2015." Geneva.
Vickstrom, Erik. 2014. "Pathways into Irregular Status among Senegalese Migrants in Europe." *International Migration Review* 48(4): 1062-99.
Villegas, Paloma E. 2012. "Assembling and (Re)marking Migrant Illegalization: Mexican Migrants with Precarious Status in Toronto." PhD. Dissertation, Department of Sociology and Equity Studies, Ontario Institute for Studies in Education, University of Toronto.
Yuval-Davis, Nira. 1997. "Women, Citizenship and Difference." *Feminist Review* 57: 4-27.

CHAPTER SEVEN
On the Role of Race and Gender in the Study of Migrant Adaptation in Canada: Comment on Boyd and Landolt

Salina Abji

Monica Boyd establishes that, on average and net of other factors, second-generation members of most Canadian visible minority ethnic groups attain a higher occupational standing than do third and later generations of White Canadians. Significantly, however, exceptions to this pattern exist. Arab, Latin American, and Black Canadians of the second generation attain significantly lower occupational scores than do members of the White third-plus generation (see Table 5.2, page 74). Due to space limitations, Boyd says little about possible reasons for these exceptions, so I want to offer a few remarks on this subject.

Numerous sociological studies document persistent racism in Canada's educational institutions, criminal justice system, and labour market (Basok 2002; Bernhard, Landolt, and Goldring 2009; Bhuyan, Korteweg, and Baqi 2016; Chan and Mirchandani 2002; Galabuzi 2006; Satzewich and Liodakis 2003). Such discrimination may well account for attenuated occupational attainment among second-generation visible minority Canadians who self-identify as Arab, Latin American, and Black.

American research shows that Latin American residents may also experience discrimination based on perceived illegality too. In fact, such discrimination extends to American citizens of Latin American origin, including those who are born in the United States; many teachers, police officers, social service agency workers, and others continue to see American citizens of Latin American origin as unauthorized residents (Gamino and Bustamante 2016; Michaels 2016; Prieto 2016). The degree to which other racial minorities in the United States and Canada are seen as unauthorized residents, even after attaining citizenship, needs to be further investigated.

Boyd also notes that Black and Latin American men are less likely to attain a bachelor's degree than are White third-plus generation men (see page 67, note 4). Apparently this difference does not exist for women. One reason for the gender difference might involve gendered dimensions of parental control. An ethnographic study of Vietnamese-American communities found that the higher educational attainment of second generation women compared to men was due in part to parents exercising greater control over daughters relative to sons (Zhou and Bankston 2001). Perhaps such gender differences in parental control operate in the case of Black and Latin American Canadians too. Another explanation for the gender difference in educational attainment may be linked to the disproportionately large number of Black and Latin American men who are punished in the school system and criminalized outside it (Ferguson 2001). These are speculations on my part. Clearly, we need more research that focuses on the intersection of race and gender in the study of second generation mobility.

Patricia Landolt adds grist to my mill insofar as she demonstrates that the structure of the Canadian immigration system is homologous with other Canadian institutions in terms of racial bias. She focuses on temporary migrants, who are often left out of studies of immigrant integration, in part because they were never intended to be integrated in the first place. Landolt demonstrates that we used to have a two-track immigration system—one track for permanent residents leading to citizenship, the other for temporary residents leading to removal. Now we have a two-track, two-step immigration system in which temporary residents who survive a difficult and protracted probationary period may in some cases enter the track of permanent residency and citizenship. However, enduring that probationary status has long-term, negative consequences for the life-chances of track switchers. Moreover, Landolt presents data showing that migrants' legal transitions are in practice more uncertain and uneven than presumed by the formal two-track, two-step structure laid out in federal policy.

We know that racialized migrants from the global south are substantially overrepresented among refugee claimants and other temporary-entrance categories (Goldring, Berinstein, and

Bernhard 2009). Recent research on conditional permanent residency also shows that sponsored spouses from Muslim-majority countries must endure longer wait times than those experienced by sponsored spouses from Muslim-minority countries (Bhuyan, Korteweg, and Baqi 2016). The great majority of sponsored spouses are women. We thus see not only institutional racism in our immigration system but also the interaction of race and gender in producing outcomes, just as we do in other Canadian institutions.

While Landolt performs a valuable service by drawing attention to the temporary residency system, she pays less attention to variation in the way different categories of temporary residents are treated. For example, I strongly suspect that the risk of deportation is much lower for international students than for temporary foreign workers. Regulatory paths have recently been cleared for international students to become permanent residents (Shen 2016). In contrast, from April 2011 until December 2016 the federal government stipulated that temporary foreign workers could be employed in Canada for a maximum of four years and then had to wait another four years before they could re-apply to work here. The rationale for this regulation was the belief that it would encourage the use of appropriate pathways to permanent residency rather than renewing temporary permits indefinitely (Citizenship and Immigration Canada, 2011; 2016). In practice, however, the regulation intensified the insecurity of legal status and tended to push migrants underground. As this example illustrates, not all temporary residents are alike, and we require research to discern differences in their treatment and the long-term consequences of differential treatment.

Importantly, Landolt points out that data on migrants living without status in Canada are crudely estimated and a decade old. This is a major stumbling block for researchers and policy makers, particularly given that the number of migrants living without status in Canada is likely rising.

In sum, both Boyd and Landolt have uncovered important effects of race and gender in immigrant adaptation. However, rather than viewing their work as conclusive, I view it as an invitation to conduct more research on social inequality in Canada that pays attention to the effects of race, gender, and their intersection.

References

Basok, Tanya. 2002. *Tortillas and Tomatoes: Transmigrant Mexican Harvesters in Canada*. Montreal and Kingston: McGill-Queen's Press.

Bernhard, Judith K., Patricia Landolt, and Luin Goldring. 2009. "Transnationalizing Families: Canadian Immigration Policy and the Spatial Fragmentation of Care-giving among Latin American Newcomers." *International Migration* 47(2): 3-31.

Bhuyan, Rupaleem, Anna C. Korteweg, and Karin Baqi. 2016. "Criminalizing 'Marriage Fraud' at Multiple Borders—Tracing the Gendered and Racialized Effects of Crimmigration in Canada." Paper presented at the CINETS conference on Crimmigration, University of Maryland.

Bhuyan, Rupaleem, Bethany J. Osborne, and Janet Flor Juanico Cruz. 2016. "'Once you Arrive, Se Te Sala Todo' (Everything is Salted): Latina Migrants' Search for 'Dignity and a Right to Life' in Canada." *Journal of Immigrant & Refugee Studies* 14(4): 411-31.

Chan, Wendy, and Kiran Mirchandani. 2002. *Crimes of Colour: Racialization and the Criminal Justice System in Canada*. Peterborough ON: Broadview Press.

Citizenship and Immigration Canada. 2011. "Backgrounder: Four-year Limit for Foreign Nationals Working in Canada." http://www.cic.gc.ca/english/department/media/backgrounders/2011/2011-03-24.asp

_____. 2016. "Government of Canada takes early action to improve the Temporary Foreign Worker Program." http://news.gc.ca/web/article-en.do?nid=1168949&tp=1.

Ferguson, Ann Arnett. 2001. *Bad Boys: Public Schools in the Making of Black Masculinity*. Ann Arbor MI: University of Michigan Press, 2001.

Galabuzi, Grace-Edward. 2006. *Canada's Economic Apartheid: The Social Exclusion of Racialized Groups in the New Century*. Toronto: Canadian Scholars' Press.

Gamino, Eric and Juan José Bustamante. 2016. "Eres Illegal o Que? Mexican American Police Officers' Voices on Migration Policy." Paper presented at the meetings of the American Sociological Association. Seattle.

Goldring, Luin, Carolina Berinstein, and Judith K. Bernhard. 2009. "Institutionalizing Precarious Migratory Status in Canada." *Citizenship Studies* 13(3): 239-65.

Michaels, Erin. "Illegal, Violent, and Scandalous: Navigating Criminalized Citizenship in the Securitized School." Paper presented at the meetings of the American Sociological Association. Seattle.

Prieto, Samuel Gregory. 2016. "'The Sense of Law is Lost': Car Impoundments and the Racial Naturalization of Mexican Immigrants." Paper presented at the meetings of the American Sociological Association. Seattle.

Satzewich, Vic and Nikolaos Liodakis. 2013. *"Race" and Ethnicity in Canada: A Critical Introduction*. Toronto: Oxford University Press.

Shen, Anqi. 2016. "Express Entry Reforms Benefit International Students Seeking Permanent Residence in Canada." *University Affairs*, November 22. http://www.universityaffairs.ca/news/news-article/express-entry-reforms/.

Zhou, Min, and Carl L. Bankston. 2001. "Family Pressure and the Educational Experience of the Daughters of Vietnamese Refugees." *International Migration* 39(4): 133-51.

Contributors

Salina Abji is a SSHRC postdoctoral fellow in the Department of Sociology and Anthropology, Carleton University, Ottawa. Her current research focuses on immigration detention practices in Canada and the gendered and racialized politics of citizenship and belonging.

Richard Alba is Distinguished Professor of Sociology at the Graduate Center, City University of New York. His most recent book, co-authored with Nancy Foner, is *Strangers No More: Immigration and the Challenges of Integration in North America and Western Europe* (Princeton University Press, 2015).

Monica Boyd, FRSC, is Canada Research Chair in Immigration, Inequality and Public Policy in the Department of Sociology, University of Toronto. Her current research projects investigate the integration of the children of immigrants in Canada, the migration of highly skilled labor and immigrant re-accreditation difficulties, gender, racial and immigrant stratification of care workers, and recent shifts in immigration policy on care workers.

Robert Brym, FRSC, is S.D. Clark Professor in the Department of Sociology, University of Toronto. His recent research projects deals with collective and state violence in Israel and Palestine; democracy and intolerance in the Middle East and North Africa; and the social bases of 21st century social movements.

Patricia Landolt is Associate Professor of Sociology at the University of Toronto. Her recent research focuses on precarious noncitizenship as a new fault line of social inequality in Canadian society. Her SSHRC-funded project (with Luin Goldring) examines how noncitizenship influences workplace rights and experiences, and access to schooling.

Naomi Lightman is an Assistant Professor in the Department of Sociology, University of Calgary. Her research focuses on gender and care work, migrant workers, citizenship and social exclusion in Canada and in comparative perspective.

Jeffrey G. Reitz, FRSC, is Robert F. Harney Professor of Ethnic, Immigration and Pluralism Studies at the Munk School of Global Affairs and the Department of Sociology, University of Toronto. He has published extensively on immigration and inter-group relations in Canada from comparative perspectives and in 2017-18 he will be Distinguished Visiting Fellow at the City University of New York Graduate Center, completing a book on Muslim integration in France, Canada and Québec.

Index

Citizenship capital, 5–6, 51–54
Demographic transition, effect on mobility, 17–19
Ethnic identities, persistence of, 16
Express Entry System, 87–88
Federal Skilled Worker Program, 87
Gordon, Milton, 12
Headscarf bans, in France, 41
Immigrants, assimilation of, 3–4, 11ff., 13–15, 26–27, 34ff., 50ff.; educational achievement of, 6ff., 58–68; occupational achievement of, 6ff., 58–76, 105ff.; second generation experiences, 58ff.
Immigrants, economic geography of, 94ff.; economic hardship of, Canada and France compared, 43ff.; experiences of, 96ff.; political representation of, 45; religion and, 47
Immigration and Refugee Protection Act (2002), 87
Immigration system, Canadian, 85–88; racial bias in, 105–107
Immigration, annual, Canada, 1–2; attitudes toward, in Canada, 1ff., 4–56, 8, 30–31, 34–35; in Europe, 1ff., 31–32; in France, 33–34; in United States, 1ff., 31–32; trends, Canadian, 89ff.
Ishaq, Zunera, 41–42
Legal status transitions, 92, 98–99
Leitch, Kellie, 3
Lisée, Jean-Francois, 3
Live-In Caregiver Program, 97, 100
Mainstream, expansion of, 14–17
Marriage, inter-ethnic and interreligious rates of, 15–16
Mixed unions, 20–26
Multiculturalism index, 33
Multiculturalism, 30–33, 45–46, 47
Muslims, discrimination against, 5
National identification, 40ff.
Parti Québecois, 3
Precarious non-citizenship, 6–7, 81–85, 100–101
Students, international, 100
Temporary Foreign Worker Program, 86–87
Unfree labour, 85
Whites, majority status of, 16–17
Women, Muslim, labour force participation of, 44
Workforce, diversification of, 19

Made in the USA
Middletown, DE
11 September 2017